Preaching in Demonstration
of the Spirit and Power

FORTRESS RESOURCES FOR PREACHING

Preaching in Demonstration
of the Spirit and Power

JOHN MASON STAPLETON

FORTRESS PRESS

PHILADELPHIA

Library of Congress Cataloging-in-Publication Data

Stapleton, John Mason.
    Preaching in demonstration of the spirit and power.

    (Fortress resources for preaching)
    1. Preaching. I. Title.
    BV4211.2.S723   1987   251   86-46424
    ISBN 0-8006-1146-2

2981E87   Printed in the United States of America   1-1146

To
Cynthia, my wife,
and to
Catherine, Mark, and David,
our children

Contents

Preface

All I have is a voice
To undo the folded lie . . .
(W. H. Auden,
"September 1, 1939")[1]

We may not be as destitute as Auden felt that sad and lonely September night in a New York City bar, but his words resonate within us because they recall to us the miracle of preaching: that our voices, even ours, can bring to expression what God did in Jesus Christ, that the sounds of faith's first proclaimers can reverberate through time and take shape in the sounds of our own tongues and larynxes. Sheer miracle! We are not so destitute. We have helpers, friends, colleagues, tradition, the community of faith. And we have the Word of God.

This book shares my discoveries concerning the miracle of that Word in the course of fifteen years as a parish minister and another eleven years as a member of seminary faculties. The encompassing nature of that statistic constrains me to acknowledge, in addition to those to whom the book is dedicated, the substantial involvement in these discoveries of my dear, now–deceased, grandmother, my parents, my colleagues in ministry, my former students, my faithful congregations. Over and over again, they have taught me that we may preach, at least every once in awhile, as did Emily Dickinson's preacher of long ago— would we knew who it was!—in a way "that scalps your naked soul," and moved her to observe:

> When winds take forests in their paws
> The universe is still.[2]

Trinity United Methodist Church   JOHN MASON STAPLETON
North Myrtle Beach, South Carolina
The Season of Easter

NOTES

1. W. H. Auden, *Selected Poems,* ed. Edward Mendelson (New York: Random House, Inc., 1979), 88.

2. Emily Dickinson, "He fumbles at your soul," in *The Poems of Emily Dickinson,* ed. Thomas H. Johnson (Cambridge: Harvard University Press, 1983).

Introduction:
The Ingredients of the
Spirit's Rhetoric

I don't think writers are sacred, but words are. They deserve respect.
If you get the right ones in the right order, you can nudge the world a
little or make a poem which children will speak when you're dead.
(Tom Stoppard, *The Real Thing*)[1]

THE HOPE

"I would give anything to preach like that," the young seminary student said. We were standing outside on the church steps just after hearing a moving, powerful sermon. When the preacher finished, the congregation had sat in prayerful silence, tears of gratitude for the truth they had heard glistening in the eyes of a few. "I hope someday I can," the student went on. You could see the yearning in his eyes even as you heard it in his voice: to stand in one pulpit after another, each congregation brought to awesome silence through the miracle of his preaching because in his words they had heard God speaking.

I have heard, time and again, other preachers share the young student's hope even as they bemoan the failure of its realization. "You can find good administrators easily enough," a bishop of the church declared to me, "but a good preacher is hard to find." "Why are there no great preachers today?" a fellow minister asked, as impatient with himself in his overly dramatic question as with the others he was judging as inadequate. I have heard both these and similar comments made while the work of ministers as a whole was affirmed. Most of us are honorable and trustworthy and morally acceptable. We counsel and do pastoral care with much skill. We plan and execute programs with success. But, overall, the consensus continues: *in our preaching we often do our poorest work.*

This book forms my response to the student's hope and all hopes

11

kindred to it. It expresses my interest in ascertaining how, in the words of Paul, we may preach "in demonstration of the Spirit and of power" (1 Cor. 2:4).

THE CENTRAL ISSUE

When Paul gave that classic description of his preaching, he was formulating and struggling with an issue that has surfaced in the church more than once when it deliberates the tasks of its preaching: Are there some techniques, strategies, models of preaching more effective than others?[2] To put the issue in the words of the Tom Stoppard quotation which begins this chapter, can preachers put the right words in the right order in such a way as to improve, if they cannot in fact guarantee, their success in nudging the world toward faith in Christ?

To the Corinthians in this instance, Paul answers with a resounding No and in specific contradiction of rhetorical skill. He has just reminded them, in the well-known first chapter of 1 Corinthians, how we humans typically measure success according to strength, wealth, social status, political and social authority, or political and social legitimacy. By these measurements, Jesus Christ was unsuccessful and ineffective. Faith in him does not arise through his conformity to them. Jesus Christ contradicts them, for in their light God's work in him appears "weak" and "foolish." God's power is manifested, faith is grounded, not in Jesus' success, but through the work of God in the Spirit, Paul declares. Likewise, speaking which might impress an audience with the right words set in the right order did not explain what had nudged the Corinthians to believe, nor could it have done so. The form of the preaching matched the content of the message![3]

The issue has surfaced, we observed, at other times in the church, just as it did in Paul's struggles with the factions in Corinth, because of the reality of Jesus Christ. If faith in him comes through a miraculous gift of the Spirit, with no other explainable "cause," including verbal eloquence and technique, does it matter then *how* we preach? Do the right words in the right order make a difference when we seek to preach in demonstration of the Spirit and of power?

THE RHETORIC OF THE SPIRIT

We are constrained, on the one hand, to join in Paul's resounding no to the question. Great preaching does not necessarily conform to standards of success that might be irrelevant to the concerns confronting us in Holy Scripture. The power of the Sermon on the Mount (Matthew 5—7) for faith cannot, for example, finally be determined by whether or not it can fill a sanctuary, or whether or not it does all to conform to rhetorical patterns.[4] Nor does a pulpiteer's winsome popularity with words prove the baptism in the Spirit of that person's preaching. When Mark reports that the common people heard Jesus "gladly" (Mark 12:37), one has no guarantee that for Mark, at least, rhetorical skill alone was the cause, whether Jesus was eloquent or not. The language of those who carry the message of Jesus Christ has often—shall we say—been uninspired and uninspiring, to say nothing of being untutored and ungrammatical. That message is rendered in the Bible, as dedicated scholars often remind us, in the untrained verbalizations of a disciple who had been a fisherman, like Peter, or of a former government worker and former crook, like Matthew, who may unrhetorically still talk out of the side of his mouth, though he no longer tells lies. Ultimately, faith does not rest upon the "cunning" a preacher might use to shape a sermon (2 Cor. 4:2).

On the other hand, to deny completely the legitimacy of the question concerning the right words in the right order would be to overstate the case. Paul himself permits us to say as much in view of recent explorations of his message from a rhetorical perspective. Both Galatians and Romans manifest the use of rhetorical devices.[5] More important for us here is his claim to the Corinthians that he addressed them in "demonstration of the Spirit and of power" (1 Cor. 2:4). The term *demonstration*, as we noted, was a technical term used in the formal study and practice of rhetoric. Paul does not imply in his use of it here that how we say what we say is unimportant but that when Christian preaching is most effective, it may manifest a certain rhetoric, an *apodeixis*, a demonstration, of its own. That is to say, we can legitimately speak of a certain "rhetoric of the Spirit" which does involve right words in the right order.

None of this is to suggest that "putting the right words in the right order" literally reflects my concern here (or Paul's) to deal with such picayune details as grammar, punctuation, sentence structure, literary organization, though, in fact, those matters in communication at times are crucial. Nor would Tom Stoppard himself want his incisive phrase taken in that literal sense. I am speaking instead of language as a whole, of the meaning that pervades it, an overall commonality of shapes and sounds and word structures, when the preaching of the gospel lays claim to them and nudges the world.

At this point we must venture beyond Paul's specific words to the church in Corinth and speak in a more systematic way concerning the rhetoric of the Spirit. For neither in Paul nor in the rest of the New Testament do we find systematic statements about preaching as we preachers are most accustomed in our time to think of it. Which is to say that the New Testament communities were not interested in conducting homiletics classes or writing books on preaching as such! *Proclamation* more aptly describes preaching in the world of the primitive church, pervasive, widespread, occurring in diverse forms, places, and utterances.[6] For the Christian community nowadays, *preaching* refers almost exclusively to the Sunday sermon in a Christian church, although its antecedents reach back into the worship of the synagogue. The Sunday sermon represents for us a tradition, highly developed, complex, even thought of as the central task of ministry. All of which is to say that I am addressing myself specifically in these pages to the proclamation of the church as it has come today to be centered in the church's typical worship.

The rhetoric of the Spirit thus manifests itself in four ingredients: (1) the dynamics of the gospel, (2) its passionate expression by the preacher, (3) artistry of form, and (4) caring for others as represented by the congregation of listeners. When these ingredients are present altogether in the Sunday sermon, there is a very real sense in which we can be sure that the Spirit is present and preaching is occurring with power.

The Gospel

The phrase "dynamics of the gospel" will occupy our specific attention in chapter 1. At the moment, however, I wish to take account of the fact that it may seem superfluous to claim that a sermon manifesting the Spirit and the power will contain the gospel. What else is a sermon for but to proclaim the "good news"? Not the manner of his speaking, we remember again Paul's admonition in the verses we have just discussed, but its content—that is, the kerygma—gave his preaching power. The gospel *is* a power-filled word.

Nevertheless, when we set forth the gospel as the first essential ingredient for preaching in the Spirit and the power, we are recognizing that in preaching we must always deal in general with the question of our faithfulness. Is a given sermon, we ask ourselves, in fact a gospel sermon? Paul himself, we must remind ourselves, had been confronted with words of power, that is to say, other "gospels" which were not the gospel itself (Gal. 1:8–9).

More immediately relevant for us now is to recall that the question of how preaching may be faithful to the gospel has been a principal subject of theological discussion for much of the twentieth century. Karl Barth comes to mind at once for many of us in the Protestant tradition. He set it as the task of theology to critique the Sunday sermon,[7] an enterprise that revitalized theology in his time and turned it into new directions, an enterprise principally elaborated into the twelve very large volumes and two "fragments" of his *Church Dogmatics:* a total of 8,716 pages, much of it in small type.

The all-embracing task of the Barthian project was to ascertain and to reaffirm a gospel that had somehow been obscured and was not being adequately or fully preached. Barth declared unto us that, tasks of translation and interpretation to the contrary, a kind of distance prevails between God and humanity, requiring not an accommodation of the gospel but its confrontation of humanity and humanity's subsequent transformation. He said at an early point in his *Church Dogmatics* that "modernist thought knows nothing finally about the fact that man in relation to God has constantly to be letting something be said *to* him, constantly listening *to* something. . . . Modernist thought . . . hears him talk to himself."[8]

Recalling the excitement of those years when the Barthian project held such commanding attention may be somewhat difficult, even for those who came then to theological maturity. Barth's theological work has been acclaimed, revised, softened, and contradicted, if not refuted by some. What remains with us across the years of the twentieth century, however, is the Barthian legacy, wherein we ask if the power of our preaching derives from the gospel rather than from mere rhetorical power. Agreement or disagreement with Barthian theology is not the point in this connection. To the point is the fact that in the closing years of this century we preachers are inheritors of Barth's renewed sense of obligation to ascertain the faithfulness of preaching to the gospel it serves. "Preaching," Barth declared, "takes place in obedience to the will of God . . . the preacher can adopt no attitude other than that of a man to whom everything is given."[9] I believe most of us would agree that something must be said *to* us as we strive to preach: a Word, to put it succinctly, from God. When we are most loyal to the gospel, that is the word of power we care most about.

Passionate Expression

A second essential ingredient required for preaching in the Spirit and the power is the preacher's passionate expression, by which I mean essentially the quality of the preacher's oral delivery. When passion is expressed in the preacher, it kindles in turn excitement in the community of listeners. Mention of this ingredient immediately takes us one step away from Barth, who, having held, in his earlier days at least, that preaching properly originated in divine revelation, continued that such preaching had "nothing to do with the preacher's convictions, or his earnestness, or his zeal."[10] I do not know if most preachers today would make a similar statement, though, in any case, even its Barthian authority does not override the compelling necessity for the evocation of feelings and emotions, that is, of the passion to which the gospel lays claim.

The New Testament does not really seek to instruct us in the religious affections. However, one can hardly imagine absence of feeling, of pathos, in Jesus, for example, when he spoke about houses built on sand or on rock (Matt. 7:24–27), or in Paul with his "now is the acceptable time, now is the day of salvation" (2 Cor. 6:2). Passionate expression would seem to be an unavoidable concomitant of religious experience in any age; nevertheless, contemporary culture requires it if the gospel is to be experienced in its full power. At least in many denominations nowadays, if not elsewhere, it may be that element of the Spirit's rhetoric which is the least understood and most lacking.

A friend of mine recently argued, "What is wrong with dullness and lack of sensationalism in preaching?" My reply was that nothing is really wrong with such preaching. Dullness is surely not *sinful,* I argued, though I daresay a dull preacher may be preaching the gospel while yet committing a certain emotional heresy! Nor is a plea for passionate expression to be taken as a suggestion for pulpit sensationalism. We preachers are not in a race with the world of entertainment, including its extravagances. It is, however, an appropriate concern to inquire into the affections the gospel can stir and what their expression involves in a culture that, to say the least, does not lack in opportunities for excitement and sensational experience. I have the impression, furthermore, that when the laity of the church plead, as so often they do, for better preaching, they are really pleading for a preacher who dares to feel the gospel message as though "overwhelmed," "caught up," "inspired," or whatever other words one might find in our language to describe the expression of passion.

Attention to the meaning and, yes, even the cultivation of what I have referred to as "passionate expression" goes neglected in many otherwise brilliant seminary curricula and by dedicated, practicing preachers. "Artists do not shout at us," Elizabeth Achtemeier declares, "nor do they engage in unbridled emotion—a truth most contemporary rock entertainers have, incidentally, never absorbed. The preacher can profit from imitating that emotional and oral restraint. I often need to remind homiletics students that they cannot attempt to grip a congregation with excitement throughout an entire twenty-minute sermon."[11] My own opinion, aside from how one judges artists and rock singers, differs. Precisely, the fault of too many preachers lies in their failure to explore the ecstatic concomitants of the gospel they preach, notwithstanding that obtrusive shouting or screaming are in general, if not always, out of place in pulpit expression.[12] Thus the goal of chapter 2 is to clarify and illuminate the issue with some suggestions for its appropriate resolution. The right words in the right order, even gospel words, are impeded in their effect unless they are delivered in the passionate mode. The right words in the right order can be wrongly uttered! The wrong words in the wrong order can be rightly uttered!

Artistry of Form

The third ingredient, the artistic form of the sermon, has attracted much attention over the last few years in reflections about preaching. *Artistry*, as I am thinking of it, refers to the style or way in which a sermon is composed, to the arrangement and shape of its elements. Obviously, a close relationship obtains with passion, for the way a sermon is organized has much to do with the way it will be expressed through the sound and movement of the preacher. Nevertheless, in the artistry of the sermon, we do indeed focus most directly upon putting the right words in the right order.

We have seen already that a central issue, theologically speaking, revolves around the propriety of such artistic, that is to say, rhetorical, considerations. Cannot God, the question has sometimes been put in the homiletical tradition, make God's message perfectly clear without rhetorical devices? Artistic or rhetorical considerations—undue concern over putting the right words in the right order—have at times seemed to suggest a lack of faith, a denial of divine grace, that does not depend upon human achievement, even in the making of a sermon.

A more subtle issue of artistry has emerged in more recent scholarly interest in the Bible as literature. One speaks, for example, of preaching as "story"[13] or in terms of "plot."[14] An anthology on "preaching biblically"[15] has been produced, but, in keeping with the trend, the anthology does not present us with preaching as discursive treatments of biblical texts; we read, instead, how the literary shapes of biblical texts may themselves shape sermons. What, in short, has given the artistic issue a distinctive turn in preaching is a claim that the Word of God itself requires such literary treatment.[16] In chapter 3, we give some attention to how our sermons may be more appropriately shaped, artistically speaking, according to that rhetoric by which the Word communicates in the Spirit and the power. Otherwise, a sermon may manifest theological aptitude, be infused with a verve that can only be described as passion, but, lacking artistry, fall short of the Spirit's requirements.

Caring for Others

The fourth ingredient belonging to the rhetoric of the Spirit and the power is the caring of the preacher for others, especially as gathered in the preacher's congregation. I mean by this a sense prevalent in the congregation that the preacher is reaching out to them in love, that real communication is occurring. I daresay that when we concentrate upon the improvement of our preaching, preachers tend to think mainly of doctrine or artistic style, even passion, forgetting to ask about our caring for the people *to* whom and *at* whom we often preach. And yet, we are compelled over and over again by the classic words of the apostle, who spoke of his own demonstration of preaching in the Spirit and the power, but still declared: "If I speak in the tongues of men and of angels, but have not love, I am a noisy gong or a clanging cymbal" (1 Cor. 13:1). In the categories I have been delineating: Though I may speak doctrinal truth with overpowering intensity, in the artistry of parables, of stories, of other, clever language shapes, and have not love, I am nothing.

Pronouncements have often been made, formally or informally, to the effect that effective preaching includes an act of pastoral care. Harry Emerson Fosdick marked an important development in the theory of preaching when he spoke of preaching as pastoral counseling en masse.[17] Later developments called such preaching into question. Theologically, the definition seemed to limit the gospel to the answering of human needs and questions when, in fact, as my own dear teacher, Paul Scherer, asserted more than once, the gospel itself had questions of its own with which the preacher must address the human situation and that might alter our definition of human need![18] From the perspective of pastoral care theory itself, pastoral care preaching seemed an enterprise at odds with itself. Preaching, almost by the very nature of the case, seemed authoritarian rather than liberating, monological rather than dialogical, not a way to be *with* persons as good pastoral care always requires.[19]

Such theological and methodological issues are indeed important. But in my concern here they are not completely on target. The main issue is more subtle. I have already spoken of it as the preacher's "reaching out." Another way to state it is to hear the subtle difference between "pastoral care" and "pastoral caring." The one tends to suggest principles, procedures, and a specific encounter. The other evokes the subtleties of the minister's attitude infusing every situation, including those situations where the minister functions as preacher. In listening to tapes of Fosdick, for example, even now, it is easy to imagine a "reaching out" explaining a considerable portion of his great appeal.

Chapter 4 of this volume explores more deeply how preaching may manifest caring as I have attempted to introduce it here. Suffice it to say that preaching may dazzle and inspire with all the right words in the right order and fail to fulfill the promise of the gospel because it does not communicate caring. It is as though the great music of the gospel were to be played, its rhythms and sounds correctly executed, but without a certain charisma in the player. The preacher's charisma of love is crucial. Without it, we may have rhetoric, which speaks with huge effect—after all, dictators, politicians, and hucksters have often done no less. But it is not a rhetoric of the Spirit.

Preaching in the Spirit and the Power: The Full Sermon

To make a judgment about the millions of sermons preached and yet to be preached is risky, requiring an unobtainable mass of evidence! It is, however, probably safe to say that no sermon has or ever will be perfect! Yet, all of us have a sense that certain sermons we have preached or heard were more effective than others. And, in any case, we need certain standards by which that effectiveness can be measured.

Obviously, a message inextricably involved with the "foolishness of God [which] is wiser than men" and the "weakness of God [which] is stronger than men" (1 Cor. 1:25), as Paul rightly declared, requires more than rhetorical technique and manipulation: the right words in the right order. But when we do not ask, given our faithful attempts to speak the gospel, how we sound and shape the words of our preaching, we are, rhetorically speaking, failing to witness to the very meaning of the incarnation itself, wherein God's self-revelation takes human form in Jesus. In ministry one rightly and appropriately accommodates to the human situation even as God does in Jesus. In Christian communication this means one's communication rightly and appropriately takes the characteristics of the human situation where communication occurs: its language, its forms of thought, its cultural styles. Asking, therefore, how the Word of God might form itself into our human words has as much value as any other question concerning how the Word became "flesh" (John 1:14).

And yet, even when theological integrity and the legitimacy of theological concern are properly considered, what we have heretofore described as caring still requires our attention. Indeed, the matter has been stated compellingly by one of the church's finest rhetoricians and preachers. After his own deliberations over the practicalities of Christian communication, Saint Augustine concluded with a reminder that a "good" (in our term *caring*) life is preferable to great speech. Let the one whose eloquence is poor, he contended, "order his life," not only for his own regard, but "also so that he offers an example to others, and his way of living may be, as it were, eloquent speech."[20]

Each ingredient of the Spirit's rhetoric as we have reviewed them has a place in our thinking about Christian communication, even as they pose issues in their relation with one another. My own conviction is that preaching more likely occurs in *demonstration* of the Spirit and the power when these ingredients come together in the same sermon and at the very least provide simple, yet legitimate, tests of preaching effectiveness. "Why are there no great preachers today?" I earlier quoted my friend. And the answer does not lie only in our failure to be faithful to the kerygma as content. Nor can we blame it on our failure to arrange our words skillfully. Nor is it just in our failure to manifest God's love to a congregation. We achieve a measure of preaching greatness to the extent that we bring these ingredients into the rich mixture they make when they are present together. For such a mixture, it is not unreasonable to appropriate the biblical admonition to "let the word of Christ dwell in you *richly*" (Col. 3:16, my italics).

When my friend asked about the great preachers of *today*, he suggested a kind of longing many preachers may have for the past, when, somehow, we may often imagine, preaching was a more successful form of communication. Did his question sound the longing felt by every generation who must assume the responsibilities formerly exercised by their mothers and fathers in the faith? Raising further the question whether the past was ever as great as we thought it was? His question has caused me to recall my own homiletical models from earlier years. To name them all here would be to no purpose. I am, nevertheless, willing to say that, for all their imperfections, at their best they richly blended the gospel, forms of its expression, and pastoral caring. Their legacy deserves our work to preserve it.

In the pages that follow, my task will be to risk offering a statement concerning each of the ingredients of the Spirit's rhetoric as I have already named them, to the end that the greatness of God's work in Jesus Christ may resound—in the right words, in the right order, and with love.

NOTES

1. Tom Stoppard, *The Real Thing* (Winchester, Mass.: Faber & Faber, 1983), 54.

2. Saint Augustine, trained in the rhetorical skills of his time and impressed by the rhetorical skill of Bishop Ambrose, would later give it classic systematic expression in *On Christian Doctrine* (trans. D. W. Robertson, Jr. [New York: Liberal Arts Press, 1958]): "For since by means of the arts of rhetoric both truth and falsehood are urged, who would dare to say that truth should stand in the persons of its defenders unarmed against lying, so that they who wish to urge falsehoods may know how to make their listeners benevolent, or attentive, or docile in their presentation, while the defenders of truth are ignorant of that art?" (1:118). An exemplary contemporary statement among several others we could cite comes from Eugene L. Lowry, *The Homiletical Plot: The Sermon as Narrative Art Form*, (Atlanta: John Knox Press, 1980), 5: "If we could just transform our intuitions into articulate forms regarding what it is that happens in our best preaching, we could *cause* it to happen by design." Yngve Brilioth, in *A Brief History of Preaching*, trans. Karl E. Mattson (Philadelphia: Fortress Press, 1965), presents a historical perspective: "One of the marks of spiritually impoverished times is too great a concern for external form. It will also become apparent, however, that the rhetorical task is by no means unimportant" (p. 61).

3. Cf. Hans Conzelmann, *1 Corinthians: A Commentary on the First Epistle to the Corinthians*, trans. James W. Leitch, Hermeneia (Philadelphia: Fortress Press, 1975), 53.

4. George Kennedy, *New Testament Interpretation Through Rhetorical Criticism* (Chapel Hill: Univ. of North Carolina Press, 1964), observes upon concluding a rhetorical analysis of the Sermon on the Mount: "Matthew says that the original audience was astounded at the speech. It has continued to startle and challenge readers for two thousand years" (p. 63).

5. Cf. Hans Dieter Betz, *Galatians: A Commentary on Paul's Letter to the Churches in Galatia*, Hermeneia (Philadelphia: Fortress Press, 1979), 14–15, 23–25. Also, W. Wuellner, "Paul's Rhetoric of Argumentation in Romans," *Catholic Biblical Quarterly* 38 (1976): 330–51.

6. Cf. Gerhard Kittel, ed., *Theological Dictionary of the New Testament* (Grand Rapids: Wm. B. Eerdmans, 1965), 3:702–3. In his article on *kerussein*, Gerhard Friedrich reminds us how at least thirty-four Greek words in the New Testament resound with the sense of "proclamation," each, to be sure, with its own more precise signification.

7. Karl Barth, *Church Dogmatics* I/1: *The Doctrine of the Word of God*, ed. G. W. Bromily and T. J. Torrance (Edinburgh: T & T Clark, 1960), 91.

8. Ibid., 68. Italics mine.

9. Karl Barth, *The Preaching of the Gospel*, trans. B. E. Hooke (Philadelphia: Westminister Press, 1963), 16.

10. Ibid., 18. The last fragment in the *Church Dogmatics*, however, *The Christian Life*, IV/4:IV, does present us with a section on passion, which Barth understands as a "zeal" for the "honor" of God, and which distinguishes a "bad sermon" from a "good" one (p. 115). Obviously, without denying a certain connection, Barth's concern here had nothing to do with passion as I am seeking to deal with it in this volume. He hoped (p. 115) that it "will not be confused with emotional and rhetorical enthusiasm." My own interest (cf. chap. 2) has to do with exploring the connection between the truth of the gospel and its oral proclamation, notwithstanding that the connection may involve something akin to "enthusiasm."

11. Elizabeth Achtemeier, *Creative Preaching: Find the Words* (Nashville: Abingdon Press, 1980), 34–35.

12. I am thinking here of *ecstasy* as used by Paul Tillich, *Systematic Theology*, vol. 1 (Chicago: University of Chicago Press, 1951). Tillich said: "It is obvious that ecstasy has a strong emotional side. But it would be a mistake to reduce ecstasy to emotion. In an ecstatic experience, emotion (like reason) is driven beyond itself" (1:114).

13. Edmund A. Steimle, Morris J. Niedenthal, Charles J. Rice, *Preaching the Story* (Philadelphia: Fortress Press, 1980).

14. Cf. Lowry, *Homiletical Plot*, no. 1.

15. Don M. Wardlaw, ed. *Preaching Biblically* (Philadelphia: Westminster Press, 1983).

16. This is the discovery elucidated, for example, by Northrop Frye, *The Great Code: The Bible and Literature* (New York: Harcourt Brace Jovanovich, 1981), 4–5. Otherwise, the literature currently reaching us regarding the linguistic and literary characteristics of the Bible is endless.

17. Harry Emerson Fosdick, *The Living of These Days* (New York: Harper & Brothers, 1956), 94.

18. Paul Scherer, *The Word God Sent* (New York: Harper & Row, 1965), 70.

19. Cf. Donald Capps, *Pastoral Counseling and Preaching: A Quest for an Integrated Ministry* (Philadelphia: Westminster Press, 1980), esp. chap. 1.

20. Augustine, *On Christian Doctrine*, 1–166.

1
The Gospel

To listen, or not listen, as a poorly paid but resplendently robed man strives to console us with scraps of ancient epistles and halting accounts, hopelessly compromised by words . . . surely in all democracy there is nothing like it. (John Updike, "Packed Dirt, Churchgoing, A Dying Cat, A Traded Car")[1]

That preaching which demonstrates the Spirit and power will contain the gospel is a true but difficult and challenging assertion, for we inevitably find ourselves yearning and straining to say more in explanation of what indeed it *means* to preach the gospel. In the first place, adequate articulation of our deepest longings, affections, and commitments confronts us with what may seem at times an almost impossible task. One thinks here of the common phrase in a moment of tragedy or ecstasy: "Words fail to express . . . " A satisfactory statement of what we have known and experienced in the gospel comes no less easily. T. S. Eliot's lines, though penned for a different context, describe the challenge and frustration of it:

Because one has only learnt to get the better of words
For the thing one no longer has to say, or the way in which
One is no longer disposed to say it. And so each venture
Is a new beginning, a raid on the inarticulate
With shabby equipment always deteriorating
In the general mess of imprecision of feeling,
Undisciplined squads of emotion . . .[2]

Other reasons for the difficulty presented by our primary assertion relate more specifically to the preacher's professional training and sensibilities. I am thinking here, for instance, of the questions posed for faith by modern biblical criticism, despite our use of it for the past two or three centuries, a use that to many preachers has repeatedly proved its value.[3] Only one such question which directly affects sermon preparation need concern us here: the pluralism within belief as expressed in faith's basic text. Among many instances of that pluralism, we have become aware, for example, that Mark, or whoever took his name, shaped and arranged the Gospel of Mark from his own special perspective. The same is true of Matthew and Luke and the Gospels bearing their names. Or the Gospel of John, we are told with a plausibility difficult to refute—if in fact we wanted to—does not contain the words of the historical Jesus. "Justification by faith" is a doctrine less central, we are told, in Paul's Corinthian letters than in the letter written to Rome. Many conclude, moreover, that in neither of these documents does the teaching of Jesus or the details of his life seem crucial. The Letter of James, to use yet another example, urges works along with faith to the extent that one may wonder if the author properly understood faith or was in danger of distorting its true meaning.

The preacher who ponders these diverse witnesses can hardly avoid some struggle with the decision over which may have more authority for preaching and why.

Another problem relating to the preacher's professional training and sensitivities involves what a New Testament scholar interested in preaching has described as the "theological chaos" that characterizes our contemporary situation.[4] We may wonder in this connection if an age of compelling theological clarity ever really did exist. Nevertheless, we think of, say, the Augustinian era, or the Reformation, or liberalism. Speaking for myself as one who grew to professional maturity in the late fifties and early sixties, a certain theological order or ethos did seem to prevail. But in any case it prevails no longer. If one asked, what is the theological order now prevailing? the question would not admit of a compelling answer, unless one responded "pluralism," which would simply underscore our earlier contention while giving it a softer answer than chaos. There is indeed a *Blessed Rage for Order*[5] in the midst of what to preachers or to others may be disorder in the household of faith itself.

I spoke in the introduction of the Barthian legacy that remains with us, namely, a sense of obligation to ascertain the faithfulness and obedience of our preaching to the gospel we seek to serve. This was the stance that led Barth to declare that theology (in his word *dogmatics*) constitutes the "test" to which the church puts its proclamation. That our proclamation requires "testing" is the legacy, I have dared to say, most of us agree on. But that is to bring us into the aforementioned chaos, beginning with the demise of Barth as the dominant theological voice of our age, by whose theology, I dare also to say, few would want in every instance to measure their preaching. Is, then, even a modicum of certitude available that we have infused our sermons with the gospel in such a way as to manifest the presence of the Spirit and power?

Neither the challenge of declaring our Christian experience and conviction nor the uncertainties caused by biblical pluralism and theological chaos obviates the necessity of our commitment as preachers to some understanding and explanation of what preaching the gospel really means to us. To live represents in itself a commitment that life, even miserable life, is better than death. Hungry, oppressed, imprisoned, suffering, failing persons who keep fighting to live are evidence. Furthermore, even if life is not miserable, we live it out of commitments, out of decisions, though they may be unorganized and unreflective. Commitments and decisions are unavoidable to selfhood, a matter of which the Kierkegaardian legacy continues to remind us. The better then to have clarity about what those decisions and commitments are, even as we stand ready to revise or change them.

Likewise, in our preaching as in our larger lives, we cannot avoid commitments and decisions, notwithstanding our struggles with appropriate words, the consistency or inconsistency of faith's primary, but pluralistic, text, and the raging for theological order. We are always *choosing* this day what the gospel really is which we serve. Indeed, its operation in the realm of commitments and decisions, of life–and–death options, is precisely what distinguishes preaching from its related disciplines. To risk a certain overstatement to make the distinction clear: both theology and exegesis are, ultimately, reflective activities of faith, in which alternatives are presented. Although it may involve reflection, every act of preaching at last represents an alternative *actually chosen* as crucial to the meaning of faith.

The issues of our original assertion thus confront us again. We must make a "raid on the inarticulate" and ask how we may still preach a gospel with power, despite its being grounded in a pluralistic tradition and in this day of theological disorder.

THE NEW TESTAMENT AS PARADIGM

The various expressions or viewpoints concerning faith that the New Testament contains have already briefly required our attention. Committed scholarship has informed us over and over again that faith's basic document presents us with writings of various genres, often transcribed from earlier, oral tradition, written by identifiable persons in some instances, by unidentifiable persons in others, each of whom wishes to make a point concerning the gospel. Each writing speaks from a certain bias, makes a claim about Jesus Christ and implies thereby, if it is not explicitly declared, a claim upon the audience, both then and now. Which is a long way of saying that the New Testament itself is a book of preaching or, dare we say, preaching*s?* For, as I also stated, preaching always manifests an attitude of decisiveness and commitment. It may require, presuppose, and stimulate reflection, but it is also more than reflection. Let us approach the New Testament then as a book of preaching and inquire how it might function as a paradigm to help us give expression to the gospel that, in preaching, we seek to serve.

Two distinguishable but inextricably related elements inform the New Testament as a book of preaching. The first involves what I shall call here the *fact* of Jesus. I mean the word *fact* as a composite term that includes his life, his death, and, however confusing their descriptions of it may be, what for the New Testament communities was the actuality of his resurrection. This composite fact *happened* and, like a boulder set in a flowing stream, forever affected the flow of time.

The Gospel generally considered to have been first composed, Mark, provides an immediately handy illustration when it opens with, "The beginning of the gospel of Jesus Christ, the Son of God" (Mark 1:1). Mark does not begin with propositions such as, for example, "Here are ten things to believe concerning God," or with a discursive statement about an intellectual or spiritual problem. He declares rather that the gospel of Jesus Christ is a happening, a fact, and then goes on to narrate other facts belonging within that all–encompassing one, concluding with Jesus' death and resurrection.

To call the composite fact *gospel,* that is, "good news," demonstrates, however, a second element: that the happening was interpreted. But not only by Mark. For the remainder of the New Testament as well, we have to do with the inextricable combination of Jesus both as fact and as an *interpretation* of fact. The Jesus fact, including his life, death, and resurrection, is that entity with which his early interpreters grappled and upon which they grounded their expressions of the meaning they discovered in it for their various times and places.

Upon a happening which to unbelievers in the ancient world was a minor incident, the New Testament communities would erect vast premises of hope, salvation, love, faith—to list only a few items in their bold vocabulary. Such premises were, moreover, uttered and re-uttered, then scribbled down, circulated, finally collected and passed on as a "testament" in the framework of stories, accounts, pronouncements, dialogues, bits of hymns, some letters or fragments thereof. These were written, said one in a sentence that, nevertheless, says it for them all, "that you may believe that Jesus is the Christ, the Son of God, and that believing you may have life in his name" (John 20:31).

THE DYNAMICS OF THE PARADIGM

One of the signal contributions of biblical scholarship for the preaching of the gospel has been the discovery of the dynamic interaction in the New Testament between the Jesus fact and the interpretations that figure both in the reporting of the fact and the statements of the fact's meaning. In searching for an image of this interaction, I have found myself unable to avoid a recollection from my student days of visual metaphors portraying the dynamics of the atom: ceaseless interaction within the atom's interior of such things as nucleus, electrons, protons, neutrons, all together containing great potentials of energy and power. Recognizing the subtleties it may ignore, even as a dramatist may exercise "dramatic license" to express a truth, I shall cheerfully take a "preacher's liberty" and rise to a generalization in this connection. The so-called Jesus fact has its major components in his life, death, and resurrection. My specific generalization is this: in the dynamic interaction between fact and interpretation, the components of the fact exercised a corrective operation upon the early Christian conscience. A given component of the fact refuses to be ignored, requires attention, imposes itself, and thus forces a new interpretation of the meaning of the Jesus fact itself.

Nowhere do we find a more impressive example of this corrective function than at the point of Jesus' death. If we look once more at the

Gospel of Mark, for instance, we are reminded of how the earliest Christians experienced and taught and spoke of Jesus as a worker of miracles.[6] At least, in the community Mark originally addressed, this was apparently the predominant understanding. Moreover, Mark suggests that Jesus' wonders were clearly all to the good, not to be construed as merely magical tricks. His healing as reported therein demonstrates his power to forgive sins (Mark 2:9–11), to cast out demons (1:34). Indeed, the entire first section of Mark as a whole reports the miracles as Jesus, the Son of God, in victorious conflict against destructive powers. Then in chapter 8 we come upon a dialogue with Peter, who, no doubt, speaks in the Gospel for the church of that time in its struggle to entertain even a hint that the Son of God, the Christ, "must suffer many things, and be rejected by the elders and the chief priests and the scribes, and be killed, and after three days rise again" (8:31).

An analysis of the cause of the resistance uttered by Peter to a suffering, crucified Christ need not preoccupy us here. Beyond the normal human reactions to personal suffering, crucifixion, and death—a certain explanation, surely, in themselves!—we do not know what or who in the church of Mark's day provoked the question of why it was "necessary"[7] that the Messiah should suffer and die. That Jesus did die in a brutal, public execution was the unavoidable *fact*, and Mark's Gospel forcefully demonstrates its powerful interaction with the Christian conscience in trying to interpret the meaning of it against the popular view of Jesus as simply a worker of wonders. Furthermore, those who would be a part of his group are warned that they must themselves suffer by taking up a cross and going where he goes (8:34). To "follow" Jesus is a far more appropriate response than religious feelings which, though not improper, are almost beside the point.[8]

Similar resistance or, more accurately, a certain destructive thoughtlessness, pervaded the attitude of the Corinthian church toward Jesus' death and reveals a central issue in Paul's Corinthian correspondence.[9] Persons in that church in a certain sense accepted Jesus' death. Much more important for them, however, was the resurrection, experienced in the ecstasy of the Spirit's presence and in their speaking in tongues. The death of Jesus was for many Corinthians a strictly past event, and they lived and thought of themselves as somehow living in a resurrected state, even as Jesus himself now lived. They ate, thought, worshiped, and played in eschatological bliss, to the degree that they may have imagined themselves as beyond dying. They apparently presumed that in baptism they had been taken up into an existence beyond death and had arrived at the final consummation.

Living in eschatological bliss, however, did not deter them from behavior that Paul denounced. They had divided into hostile groups and indulged in name-calling (1 Cor. 3:1–4). They were selfish to the point of refusing to share their food with the poor who came hungry to the Lord's Supper (1 Cor. 11:20–21). They did not care to ponder the implications of the faith for their sexual behavior (1 Cor. 5:1ff.), and, though they spoke in tongues and were wise and gloried in their faith, they did not have love (1 Cor. 13:1ff.). Paul's sarcastic comments tell us they claimed to be "filled" already, to be "rich," ruling like "kings" (1 Cor. 4:8), when, in fact, whatever they had in their new life had come to them as a gift (1 Cor. 4:7).

Paul's response to this state of affairs manifests, just as we saw it in another context in Mark, the corrective function of the fact of the death of Jesus. Paul's own thinking exemplifies the hold of that component belonging to the great fact upon himself. The burden of his message to the Corinthians has it that, although Jesus has been raised from the dead, he is still *as* the risen One the *Crucified.*[10] Recognition and acknowledgment of the death of Jesus in just this way must have profound impact upon their faith and life. Christians are called, not to a life of unworldly, eschatological bliss, but to a life of love and service in the here and now.

An additional characteristic of the dynamism of the Jesus fact now enables me to enlarge upon my generalization and visual metaphor. Not only does the New Testament exhibit how a component of the fact can exercise its corrective operation, we can also observe that a component manifests an "attraction" or "movement" toward the other components. The resurrection will not finally allow to be ignored the question of *who* rose from the dead and *why*? and thus moves the chief theologian of the Corinthian church to assert that one cannot be faithful to the meaning of Jesus' resurrection without attention to its antecedent fact, namely, his death.

But the death of Jesus moves backward, as it were, to the narrative of his life, as witnessed by the formation of the Synoptic Gospels. A Messiah who is crucified surely invites reflection upon the quality of his life. How otherwise would his disciples know what it means to follow him? What is his guidance, one might ask, to problems of suffering and death? In Mark, as we saw, if a healer is crucified, one's reflections upon the healing are inevitably altered. But, again, to read the narrative of his life simply as narrative, one experiences how the life drives forward toward his death in order that the life itself may be appropriately understood.

The Gospel of John evidences the claim of the Jesus fact to be, in fact, a *fact* when it asserts, "the Word became flesh." John's Gospel then states a meaning for the fact's various components: Jesus' life, how it was inextricably linked with his death, and even suggests that that Gospel itself is a text which somehow manifests resurrection, not the least because it utters what the happening of the Jesus fact now means for those whom the Gospel addresses.[11]

When we recall what we have previously described as the pluralism of interpretations within the New Testament concerning Jesus, it is obvious that the brute fact provides the unity of concern. The New Testament paradigm for preaching does not thus manifest for our preaching a simple unity of conceptual content; rather, *its unity may be found in the struggle of those whose writings it contains to make sense of the happening which was Jesus.*

I am aware in this connection of the issue, which continues to tax faithful scholars, concerning whether or not we are dealing in the New Testament with fact, a matter strongly urged in this chapter, or with interpretation—which some might prefer to describe as "faith"— wherein events are only *reported* of Jesus as having happened when actually the best evidence suggests they did not or cannot be verified as such. We cannot resolve the issue here any more decisively than it has been resolved elsewhere.[12] Mention of it serves rather to underscore my previous generalization of "corrective operation" and "attraction," although these descriptions do no more than touch the richness of early Christian experience allowed by the metaphor of the atom as a way to consider the dynamism New Testament preaching offers us.

I should, nonetheless, make it clear that I am not here aligning myself with a position once stated by Kierkegaard concerning the New Testament writers: "If the contemporary generation had left nothing behind them but these words: 'We have believed that in such and such a year God appeared among us in the humble figure of a servant, that he lived and taught in our community, and finally died,' it would be more that enough."[13]

Kierkegaard was correct, I believe, in his understanding that the truth of faith could neither be proved nor guaranteed by a historical fact. Nor is faith dependent upon historical research. He was incorrect, however, in not sufficiently recognizing that fact could and would exercise its impact upon faith. And that is precisely the nature of the dynamism to which I have sought to call attention. Much of what may be identified as "historical reconstruction"[14] explores how the facts of Jesus' history and the faith of its early participants interact.

PREACHING THE GOSPEL

The answer to our earlier query concerning how we may authentically and with power preach the gospel today presents itself at just this point. Preaching that is faithful to the gospel somehow will suggest, if it does not explicitly declare, the dynamism of the New Testament paradigm. The preacher stands in this instance as a servant and learner of both fact and interpretation, ascertaining how their interaction may have impact upon any given sermon or sermons, each by God's grace yet another utterance of truth born of the preacher's involvement with a "minor incident" and the sacred texts elucidating the vast premises faith has erected upon it.

We should be careful not to formalize the dynamism of the basic paradigm as it would apply to all preaching, for the unique, creative process peculiar to each preacher might be stifled, to say nothing of the uniqueness that belongs to every sermon. *The one regulative principle of preaching, however, requires that it demonstrate the grappling of the preacher with the Jesus fact and the dynamic interplay of its components.*

In addition, it is not too much to say that observance of the Christian year can encompass the full spectrum of the preacher's work and as such will express the dynamism of the New Testament paradigm. If faith's basic text exhibits the dynamism of the atom, the Christian year is its nuclear whirlwind, moving through the course of history, drawing all time into the time of Jesus, the event of the Jesus fact enclosing within the dynamic interplay of its components all other events.

The full development of what Dom Gregory Dix once called the "sanctification of time"[15] cannot be traced here. Nor can I give adequate attention to more recent developments that it involves, such as the increasing use in preaching of the *Common Lectionary*. But it can be noted that the development of the Christian year manifested the components of the Jesus fact in their corrective and attracting operations. The Christian year first moved into time with a weekly celebration of the resurrection and with an annual observance of Pentecost, which celebrated the gift of the Spirit and life lived in its presence and power. Shortly here, then there, as the church continued to occupy time and space, it came also to experience the irresistible presence of Jesus both as the Crucified and the One who lived and continues to show us the way. One legacy of this process is the celebration of the Christian year as we celebrate it today, whose force can yet draw all other time into itself and give power to preaching.

Great movements in Christian history are not easy to characterize in simplistic formulae. Some movements, however, whatever else they display, remind us of aspects of the Jesus fact that the Christian conscience could not at last ignore, and that often shaped the preaching of the time. Did not the Reformation, for example, in its concern with justification by faith confront the church with Jesus' death against a misunderstanding of the relationship between grace and the Christian life? Or was the Social Gospel movement not a plea for concern with how in obedience to the life of Jesus we ourselves should order our lives? Or, again, could theological currents in the years following the time of the Social Gospel not be reported as having flowed from discoveries of what the death and tragedy of faith's central figure tell us of the human condition? And for all the variegations of Christian experience it includes, surely more recent discussions of the Christian hope are responses to the attraction of that component of the Jesus fact where he was experienced as risen from the dead.

THE JESUS FACT AND CURRENT PREACHING

The sheer number of preachers and the sermons they preach make characterizations of preaching being carried on at a given period extraordinarily difficult. The best one can do, perhaps, involves a sense of those notions that seem popular, as much cultural analysis as one can absorb, and hard data about who and what "sells," though even these sources for characterizations might prove to be inadequate.

I venture, however, the overall observation that much preaching today in America reminds us of the situations at Corinth and in Mark's Galilee, where, in both, the death component of the Jesus fact was being ignored or at least misunderstood.

One way to elucidate this current situation is by reference to the American understanding of success. If in Corinth some Christians thought of themselves as already transmitted into glory, where there was no death, American Christians (to say nothing of other Americans) are offered the gospel as the way to health, wealth or, at least, financial solvency, job security or promotion, life without stress.

Here before me, for example, is a sermon by a well-known, even famous, pulpiteer with no awareness, not even a hint, of Jesus, as the ancient creed has it, "crucified, dead, and buried." The sermon does refer on occasion to human problems and pain, minor and severe. One wonders whether the ecstatic persons in Paul's church acknowledged as much; certainly, in Mark's church they did, as the stories in Mark of suffering persons seeking and finding help indicate. In any case, the modern preacher in this instance promises actual power through which the difficulties can be overcome and proves it by stories of success. An employer desperately needed two new employees to make a new business go. They were found, the preacher says, in answer to prayer. Another person owed several hundred dollars. He prayed to God, and the next morning two friends offered to lend him money, though he had not told them of his financial desperation. Another prayed for a wife, and within days a young woman came to him seeking work, and he knew at once she came also in response to his prayer.

Variations upon this siren theme of success are easy to find. A very noticeable, even noisy, section of believers makes much today of physical healing, reminding us of the Markan chuch. A certain difference may obtain between those who think of faith as offering success and those who focus more specifically upon the restoration of health. On occasion, however, they do become synonymous. Another variation seems to make more of human effort and attitudes than the sermon mentioned above, which resounds like magic in its stress upon almost ritualistic praying for certain benefits. On the other hand, in a land of eschatological bliss, even in the twentieth century, the magic whereby one seeks to bend omnipotent power to one's own ends hardly differs from belief in the inevitability of sheer effort and the right attitude.

Each variation rejoices in the simple guarantee of well-lived, successful existence to all who have faith.

By the implicit standards of such preaching, Jesus was a failure. So the Jesus fact moves upon the preacher to exercise its corrective operation. For Jesus, who did practice the presence of God and sought God's guidance, went to a Roman cross begging. "If it be possible, let this cup pass from me" (Matt. 26:39). On the cross itself, he was not certain of the divine presence, crying out his consciousness of the abandonment by his Father, or what for him surely seemed abandonment. The *fact* of this death of its Lord asserts itself to faith, perturbs the Christian conscience, and, in terms of the sermon we have quarreled with, somehow relates to all other failures—personal or corporate bankruptcies, disappointing courtships, broken marriages—that befell persons who yet prayed for success and were aware of the presence or absence of God. For all his good intentions and optimistic attitudes, Jesus died a brutal death, and a preacher who allowed it to work its way into consciousness would have a different sermon.

Not only would the death itself have decisive impact upon the sermon. The death of Jesus, as we earlier declared, exists in dynamic interaction with his life. He who died a "ransom for many" (Mark 10:45) also ate and drank with "tax collectors and sinners" (Mark 2:16) and gave the counsel that informed his own words and actions: "Love your neighbor as yourself" (Matt. 19:19). Paradigmatically speaking, a Christian attempts in his or her own life to give service and obedience in Jesus' name. Business, marriage, home, human relationships in general are valid subjects for prayer, but the preacher of the gospel could not avoid, if only by implication, that the courage and sacrifice of the faithful life may be a way that leads unto death (Phil. 2:8) or, certainly, to other than glorious success.

But we should remember once more that Jesus' faithfulness and our faithfulness unto death are drawn powerfully to the resurrection, when his "failure" was vindicated and overcome, and which points the way to whatever vindication and victory we ourselves may dare lay claim to.

A POSITIVE EXAMPLE

No one formula or design can guarantee an expression in preaching of the dynamics of the New Testament paradigm. Besides, I have warned how a specific design would possibly impose the creative process unique to each preacher. It will be helpful, nevertheless, as a further explanation of the process, to examine at least one sermon that, in my opinion, faithfully manifests the operations of the Jesus fact as we have described them.

The sermon is by a preacher, George Buttrick, now deceased, who at the height of his power mightily influenced the preaching of the Word. Buttrick, among other accomplishments, preached regularly for twenty-five years in New York City at Madison Avenue Presbyterian Church, and then became preacher at the Memorial Church at Harvard University. The sermon has as its text the saying best known as the Golden Rule: "Whatever you wish that men would do to you, do so to them" (Matt. 7:12).[16]

The theme of the sermon derives from the famous nomenclature associated with the text: "Is It the Golden Rule?" Putting the theme as a question for the congregation itself signals, perhaps, that the great admonition as spoken by Jesus has an ambiguity about it and, as we shall see in retrospect, begins to quiver with the dynamism of the Jesus fact.

In the introduction Buttrick orients the sermon around one who might say, in popular fashion, "My religion is the Golden Rule." In the beginning, he raises quickly the question (not raised by the other sermon we have touched upon, *and a matter that the death or "failure" of the Jesus fact allows*) whether such a "religion"—really no more than "individualistic ethics"—can deal at all with the "enigma of pain, or about life after death, much less about sin and forgiveness."[17]

The first part of the sermon following the introduction treats of possible misinterpretations of the Rule—as an argument for sheer selfishness, for example, or as regards someone who throws a "super duper cocktail party," hoping he will be invited to all the others in his neighborhood. Then Buttrick raises the question of why we credit the Rule to Christ. He makes the point that in its negative phrasing, "Whatsoever you would *not* wish," and so on, it was also uttered by Confucius, Epictetus, and Hillel.

This brings him to the second section, where the corrective function of the Jesus fact, particularly as regards Jesus' death, becomes more articulate. Indifference, coveting, sinful deeds of the past ("No man can cleanse history, or even his own memory"), self-concern—all cause us to experience the Golden Rule as "the whole burden of man's transgression." The preacher asks, "Now where has the Golden Rule led us? To a profound doctrine of the Atonement! The Golden Rule of itself is a dark burden which no man can hear, until Christ gathers it in grace."[18]

The third section of the sermon points out that the Rule as a rule tends to evoke rebellion. A saying such as this one, it is urged, does not manifest Christ as a rule giver, and we are disabused of the notion that he ever would be. At this point we observe that the preacher recognizes that the death of Christ "attracts," to use our earlier term, the life of Christ and our life in service to him. "Jesus doesn't give us a manual of directives, as if we were junior executives or 'hands' in some mammoth corporation. He doesn't bark at us as if he were our drill sergeant, and we were privates in his army."[19] Rather, he calls us "friends" and says: "This is my commandment, that you love one another as I have loved you" (John 15:12). So it is that the Rule "no longer sets our teeth on edge because it has won our hearts."[20]

The closing section of the sermon provides its own restatement of much of the description given in this chapter of New Testament dynamics. Not all sermons would need to be so specific—another matter we have touched upon. The point is nevertheless well taken. Buttrick reminds us that the Golden Rule is set in the Sermon on the Mount and that "we have no right to lift the Sermon on the Mount from the context of the whole Gospel." He characterizes the entire Gospel of Matthew as having "five double panels set between Christmas on the one side and Calvary and Easter on the other side." The Golden Rule "in the second half of the initial panel"[21] is set between Christmas and Calvary-Easter. "That is why it is blind without Christ, and burdensome without Christ."[22] After some further comment and the reporting of an incident that refers us back to the beginning question, "Is it the Golden Rule?" the preacher asks, do we ever know what is "right" until we "stand before the Cross remembering that its shadow falls on us by the light of the Resurrection?" His answer: "Yes, the Golden Rule is indeed the Golden Rule, but only because the Rule is held in the life and love of him who spoke it, who has said also: 'Love one another as I have loved you.'"[23]

One could have spoken of the Golden Rule as the essence of all good religion or of productive human relationships. The Rule could have been spoken of in more individualistic, self-serving terms, as a Rule which, carefully followed, will assure one of material and social success. In this specific sermon, the preacher links the Rule with the doctrine of the atonement, that is, with the death of Jesus, and in the last section states that the Golden Rule acquires its proper understanding from the cross. The entire sermon manifests the corrective function of the Jesus fact that in this case drives the saying of Jesus forward to his death and the love and goodness of God it signals. Moreover, the impingement of his death upon his life and our life is highlighted, and even the resurrection has brief mention.

SUMMARY

I have dared to characterize the New Testament as a dynamic witness of how the Jesus fact operates upon early Christian sensibilities, and I have promoted that dynamism as a fitting paradigm for determining the dynamics of all preaching. The dynamic works, I said, in two related ways. On the one hand, a component of the Jesus fact—his life, death, or resurrection—asserts itself, demands attention, as necessary for the comprehension of the gospel as a whole. On the other hand, the components exist in dynamic interaction toward one another, enriching and giving increased power when a sermon reflects their interaction.

The forms and expressions of this dynamism are as various as those preachers who attend to them and in the number of sermons they preach. Furthermore, one aspect of the Jesus fact may be more prominent for a while in the church's life, giving way to the other in the manner of the New Testament, or, as an observance of the Christian year itself, may require attention. Response to the dynamic claims of faith's basic text marks the first essential step to preaching in demonstration of the Spirit and power our hearts yearn for.

NOTES

1. John Updike, *Pigeon Feathers and Other Stories* (New York: Fawcett Crest Books, 1963), 170.

2. T. S. Eliot, "East Coker," in *The Complete Poems and Plays* (New York: Harcourt, Brace & Co., 1952), 128.

3. Cf. the more extensive and helpful discussion by Leander E. Keck, *The Bible in the Pulpit: The Renewal of Biblical Preaching* (Nashville: Abingdon

Press, 1978), 22–30.

4. Ibid., 45–48.

5. David Tracy, *Blessed Rage for Order: The New Pluralism in Theology* (Minneapolis: Winston Press, 1975).

6. In what follows, I am giving a summary statement of my own as gathered from various commentators upon Mark's presentation of the gospel.

7. Mark 8:31, my trans. The Greek here is *dei* and appropriately translated as "necessity" in view of the great and massive mystery of the divine purpose portrayed in Mark and the other Synoptic Gospels.

8. Cf. James Robinson, *The Problem of History in Mark* (London: SCM Press, 1962), 68–75. I am indebted to Professor Robinson's discussion which points out that for Mark "faith" is preferable to strictly religious "awe" or "fear" and is further underscored by Mark's use of "follow" as a synonym for "faith."

9. Cf. James Robinson, "Kerygma and History in the New Testament," in *The Bible in Modern Scholarship*, ed. J. Phillip Hyatt (Nashville: Abingdon Press, 1965), 123–24. The entire discussion presents an enlightening presentation of how history (in my term *fact*) and kerygma (*interpretation*) interacted in Paul's letters to Corinth.

10. Cf. for the exegetical details, William Childs Robinson, Jr., "Word and Power," in *Soli Deo Gloria: New Testament Studies in Honor of William Childs Robinson*, ed. J. McDowell Richards (Richmond: John Knox Press, 1968), 71.

11. Leander Keck ("The Flesh Becomes Word" in *Evangelism: Mandates For Action*, ed. James T. Laney [New York: Hawthorn Books, 1975], 51–66), sees in the relation of the Gospel of John to the Synoptic Gospels a clue to how Jesus as history (in my term *fact*) may be related to Jesus as interpreted history.

12. Keck provides a succinct and clear discussion (see ibid., 128–35).

13. Søren Kierkegaard, *Philosophical Fragments*, trans. David F. Swenson (Princeton: Princeton University Press, 1936), 87.

14. Cf. n. 11.

15. Dom Gregory Dix, "The Sanctification of Time," in *The Shape of the Liturgy* (New York: Seabury Press, 1983), 333–69.

16. George A. Buttrick, "Is It the Golden Rule?" in *The Twentieth Century Pulpit*, ed. James W. Cox (Nashville: Abingdon Press, 1978), 30–35.

17. Ibid., 30.

18. Ibid., 32.

19. Ibid., 33.

20. Ibid., 34.

21. Ibid.

22. Ibid., 34–35.

23. Ibid., 35.

2
Passionate Expression

It is fire that makes a difference between one man or another; it is not intelligence, it is not the mere use of words. (Joseph Parker, Preacher, City Temple, London, 1881)

PREACHING AND PASSION

A student in a preaching class of mine once expressed a common frustration. "Most sermons I hear," he said, "are full of understanding. Few are full of conviction." *Understanding* for him at that moment referred to responsible theological work, careful study of a biblical text, obedience to the correctives required by the gospel as a whole. *Conviction* for him was synonymous with passion, the word I myself prefer, because conviction suggests not only strong feeling but a feeling that expresses a conclusion of thought which has emerged from the preacher's mental struggle. *Passion* speaks less of a conclusion about which the preacher feels strongly than of a response to an object evoking a powerful emotion the preacher cannot easily avoid—a matter to which I shall soon give more attention. Passion in preaching involves the right words in the right order appropriately expressed in the preacher's voice and gestures. It concerns what we ordinarily refer to as the preacher's delivery, the manner in which a sermon comes to us off the pages of the preacher's text—if the sermon is written—or directly from the pages of the preacher's inner self. Passion lifts up the right words in the right order and sends them forth from the preacher on wings of sound.

To inquire how it is that preaching in the Spirit and power requires passion would be like asking why one exclaims over a beautiful sunset, or breaks out into song, or cheers over a touchdown. How much more also then would one expect emotionally laden responses to the One who evokes faith—whose life and death win our devotion and trouble our conscience, whose resurrection gives us hope. Feeling and the expression of feeling belong to the human species. Although it may not require passion to authenticate its truth, successful communication of the gospel may have it as a highly valuable ingredient. "I think," declared Jonathan Edwards, our most esteemed and classic American preacher in matters of religion and emotion, "an exceeding affectionate way of preaching about the great things of religion, has in itself no tendency to beget false apprehensions of them; but on the contrary a much greater tendency to beget true apprehensions of them, than a moderate, dull, indifferent way of speaking of them." He went on to conclude: "Our people do not so much need to have their heads stored, as to have their hearts touched." Moreover, their greatest need was of "that sort of preaching, that has the greatest tendency to do this."[1]

Edwards had begun his classic work of 1746 on religious experience by observing that "true religion, in great part, consists in holy affections," and gave it the famous title, *A Treatise on Religious Affections.*[2] Affections, he said, were "the more vigorous and sensible exercises of the inclination and will of the soul."[3] The affections, which in this book I have elected to call passion, belonged in Edward's view to human nature, and, most relevant for us here, have a special connection with preaching. God ordained preaching "that divine things might be impressed upon the affections of men." Scriptural commentary and exposition give us "doctrinal or speculative knowledge of the things of religion," but they do not "impress them on men's heart and affections." For *that* God had intended something else:

> God hath appointed a particular and lively application of his word to men in the preaching of it, as a fit means to affect sinners with the importance of the things of religion, and their own misery, and necessity of a remedy, and the glory and sufficiency of a remedy provided; and to stir up the pure minds of the saints, and quicken their affections by often bringing the great things of religion to their remembrance, and setting them before them in their proper colors, though they know them, and have been fully instructed in them already.[4]

Others have urged passion as a mark of more adequate Christian proclamation in the history of preaching. The Lyman Beecher Lectures on preaching at Yale provide examples. Henry Ward Beecher, who established and was himself the first lecturer in the series begun in 1871, did not use the word *passion*, but his comments were to the same point. Beecher's word in one place was *enthusiasm*. A preacher may carry the people with him without it, but, he declared, "It will be a slow process, and the work will be much more laborious." Beecher continued:

> If you have the power of speech and the skill of presenting the truth, and are enthusiastic, the people will become enthusiastic. People will take your views, because your enthusiasm has inoculated them.[5]

Other lecturers through the years spoke of "earnestness," "conviction," "a soul of flame," "vigor," "virility." Phillips Brooks declared he could not give "it" a name. "Call it enthusiasm," he suggested, "call it eloquence, call it magnetism; call it the gift for preaching." Another quoted Saint Augustine, who spoke of fervor—more necessary, said the Saint, than any endowment of intellect "to inform the understanding, catch the affections, and hence the will of his hearers." John Watson spoke of "intensity" and explained lack of it as a lack of "spiritual passion." Again, Broadus thought of "energy," that is, animation, force, and, also, used a cognate of my own word *passion*: "There must," he said, "be vigorous thinking, earnest if not passionate feeling . . ."[6] Halford E. Luccock's lectures came in 1954, seven years following the publication of the compendium from which I have drawn my earlier comments. Upon his retirement from Yale, Luccock gave the lectures and reminded his hearers that the highest tribute the eighteenth century could pay to a preacher was "pious, without enthusiasm," and immediately and strongly countered that preaching—if it stood, he said, in the apostolic succession—should obey "two of the basic laws of propaganda. First, reiteration . . . second, *passionate affirmation*."[7]

Obviously, treatment of the subject of preaching and passionate expression could be updated. In view of my earlier, introductory comments, the concern for it expressed by preachers of earlier generations strikes us with special interest. I have dared to say that somewhere along the way in more recent years the delivery of the sermon, of which I am pleading that passion is a primary ingredient, became of so much less concern. Kyle Haselden would argue in the decade following Luccock that, at a time when "public speech" was on the rise more than ever before in the history of language, "ministers, whose chief tool is the spoken word, have in general less skill and less training in oral communication than men and women in a host of other professions."[8]

To be exact, Haselden did not speak specifically of passion. But he did worry over matters of "voice" and "skills in expression," matters which seem to underscore my first observation that passion involves the preacher's voice and gestures.

PASSION AND DISCOVERY

A crucial deficiency runs consistently through most considerations of communicating the sermon with passion. It is presented as a need or an obligation. The excerpts quoted from the Beecher lectures, for example, deal with it almost totally as a necessary mode for a sermon's delivery, as though that alone would guarantee its presence and manifestation in the preacher. Recognition of the deficiency, however, will not provide its correction.

We can learn here from a cardinal rule of all good psychotherapeutic and pastoral counseling in this connection. That cardinal rule is that one cannot deny the presence of a feeling, that that feeling must, for the well-being of the counselee, be acknowledged and expressed. An obverse rule also applies: a feeling cannot be required. So far as the rule applies to the preparation and delivery of a sermon, a preacher errs in thinking of passion as simply a requirement. Theologically speaking, the error makes of feeling a matter of law when it is preeminently a matter of grace. Even as one cannot save oneself by work of the law, neither can one command intensity of feeling. How could anyone demand of John Wesley or a contemporary follower and disciple of Wesley that his or her heart be "strangely warmed"? I have, I fear, heard contemporary preachers make precisely such a demand, when in fact the warm heart of Wesley was not grounded in a command he made of himself or that anyone else made of him.

The passion of which I speak and which has theological legitimacy may be best identified as the result of a *discovery* of the reality of the gospel. It is as though one had gazed upon a scene, heard a song, listened to a story, and found one's feelings powerfully stirred, which, not incidentally, describes Wesley's Aldersgate experience. The preacher "discovers" the reality of the gospel, which in turn arouses that intense, emotional reaction we have spoken of as passion. In that sense, passion occurs as a byproduct. To be sure, the preacher has more than once heard, studied, reflected upon the gospel, but passion is evoked as the gospel is yet *re*apprehended, *re*experienced, and *re*understood—in a word, *rediscovered*.

The work and mystery of the theater help to explain the process. No actress or actor tries to manufacture feeling or emotion. Theologically speaking, we have already taken account of that as illustrating the futility of the law. Dramatically speaking, it is equally futile. When developing a stage character, the actor or actress gives attention not to the emotions of the character to be portrayed, but to the realities of the character's life: the character's private thoughts, relationships with other characters on and off the stage, the dramatic situation itself. In theatrical terms, this is known as "concentration."

The actor playing Mark Antony in Shakespeare's *Julius Caesar* will not worry about the emotions of grief and rage over Caesar's assassinated corpse.[9] He will think of the fact of Caesar himself: the loyal and close friendship they had, their battles together for Rome, the danger Caesar's death brings to political stability. The actor will behold the "bleeding piece of earth" brought "so low." He will ponder in his private moment with Caesar's corpse the knife wounds that "ope their ruby lips." He will ponder the "rent" made in Caesar's body by "the envious Casca," and the "most unkindest cut of all" made by Brutus, formerly Caesar's most loyal supporter and confidant, now his preeminent betrayer. In his concentration upon the realities of Caesar's death, the actor "becomes" Antony. The passions of grief and rage overtake him as byproducts. A part of one's work in theater *and in preaching*, both of which deal in legitimate human emotions, requires learning to discover them and to allow their expression. The preacher who concentrates upon gospel realities in this sense "discovers" the gift of passion.

DISCOVERY, INTEREST, THE PREACHER'S "INNER DANCE"

We move more deeply into our analysis of passion and discovery by asking, What makes a sermon interesting? Why do people listen to it, or what enables them to? No one, of course, can ever completely explain why we give our attention to a specific public address of any kind, or, more especially, why some addresses are more easily listened to than others. The closest we come to an explanation, however, revolves around the word *energy*. It is a favorite word in all the performance disciplines, especially the stage. In staging a drama, a director knows that the interest of an audience will center upon the place of most energy among the actors and that a dramatic piece with a proper dramatic flow will involve exchanges of energy among the characters on stage.

A further question now presses us, How does one define energy? Again, precise description always eludes us. It does involve, nonetheless, an association with movement. Where energy is, however else we think of it, movement usually occurs, and movement collects interest. Movement among characters on stage must be directed in such a way that it helps the drama rather than interrupts or impedes it, and one hopes that the movement of someone in the audience who leaves will not be a movement too diverting! And dramatic characters may be identified in part by the nature of their movements: an old woman, perhaps, with the pain of age, the majestic movement of a king, the bewildered movements of someone lost in a forest.

Discovery that issues from concentration upon a reality, be it a factor present and available to a participant in a dramatic piece or in the reality of the gospel, activates energy. It puts energy in motion, and thus moves the preacher to interesting expression. In its simplest delineation, this is the process by which passionate expression—yearned and called for by such homileticians as we have mentioned—happens.

The question may further arise here concerning how energy operates in the different situations obtaining between the stage and pulpit. After all, dialogue sermons and the like to the contrary, the preacher presents a one-person "show." Moreover, pulpit space does not admit of movement common to a stage. Nor does it need to. Nor does it necessitate attempts by the preacher to create interest by moving out from behind the pulpit or by striding up and down the church aisle. Energy may, and often does, operate with more subtlety. Discovery and the energy it activates, when they appropriately operate in the preacher, occur as the preacher's *inner* movement, which I prefer—because of the joy that belongs to the preacher's message—to speak of as an *inner dance*. The inner dance refers to that activation of energy arising from discovery by the preacher of the gospel, which a congregation does not see, but which it may certainly sense. We shall explore the place of voice and gesture later, but suffice it now to note that histrionics are beside the point—they may even be distracting.

AUTHENTIC VERSUS SPECIOUS PASSION

At this point the issue confronts us of whether or not expression communicates authenticity of passion. Admittedly, we are casting about here in the murky and not always ascertainable realm of a preacher's hidden motivations. The risk involved cannot allow us, however, to refuse making judgments concerning the truth of our feelings—or, again, concerning whether we *really* feel what we *say* we feel. The dramatist, to say nothing of the audience, well knows the difference between drama and melodrama. The swooning woman on stage who makes a show of widening her eyes, throwing her hand and head back, and fainting or pretending to faint, is a well-known example. That is melodrama, including the melodramatic sermon, where emotion and the expression of it itself become the preoccupation rather than the reality that evokes emotion.

We have reminded ourselves already of the preacher who may move out of the pulpit, up and down the aisles, or seek other ways to have effect. I am reminded of a popular television preacher who has, I have been told, sometimes been seen exhibiting himself to himself on a television monitor just prior to the airing of the service. Striking different stances, postures, and profile views before his monitored self, he leads us to gather that more is involved than a simple check to make sure that no personal dishevelment might detract from his message. The actual telecast follows with strange gestures by the preacher and ways of pronouncing words with jerks and pounces of breath, all leading us to wonder, why is he doing all this? For the sake of the gospel?

I remember yet another preacher whose facial expression and gestures were apparently planned to the last smile. Her performance was very studied; nothing seemed spontaneous. I later learned that she wrote out her sermons and arose at four o'clock on Sunday morning to prepare and practice gestures and even facial expressions for the approaching—and in this instance, the word perfectly fits—*performance.*

Popularity is not the issue here. Authenticity is. That lay persons may praise some of these performances, which in my judgment are performance aberrations, cannot be denied. The preening television preacher does indeed have a following. Other than the sometimes astounding ability of lay persons to overlook poor performance, my suspicion is that they approve such aberrations because they would rather have them than the convictionless delivery mentioned by my student. Certainly, we have no reason to suppose that authenticity would go unappreciated by the lay mind or heart. In any case, to glory in one's style or to find remarkable the way one moves in sermon delivery betrays one as a mistress or gigolo of the pulpit. The discovery that sets in motion the inner dance may be sensed by a congregation, and that is enough. Without *discovery*, all movements may come across to a congregation as false.

The entertainer in John Osborne's play by the same name describes the matter precisely, not only for himself, but for that inauthentic preacher as well: "You see this face, you see this face, this face can split open with warmth and humanity. It can sing, and tell the worst, unfunniest stories in the world to a great mob of dead, drab erks. . . . It doesn't matter because—look at my eyes. I'm dead behind these eyes."[10]

Authentic passion in a sermon occurs and gets communicated in every instance from that process of discovery that happens as one concentrates upon the reality sparking the passion. Specious passion reveals a pathology I shall not try in these pages to explain though I have my tentative opinions. The phenomenon of it, however, can be witnessed when expression, passionate or not, operates out of a different psychological dynamism, such as we have described in the examples recently given, than the discovery by the preachers of the "real thing." Without that discovery of which we have been speaking, passion is inauthentic, either full of "sound and fury, signifying nothing," or it may signify something but with the great sound and fury of the gospel drama still unexperienced in both the pulpit and the pew.

PASSION AND TURNING ON TO
THE BIBLICAL TEXT

Sermons preached in the Spirit and the power do not usually, if ever, begin with an idea in the preacher's head. Most likely, they begin at that moment when, as one reads the text to begin preparation, the hairs at the nape of the neck rise, or one catches one's breath, or whenever else one finds oneself overwhelmed by emotion. It will be a long way from the initial reactions to that moment of presentation of the sermon to a congregation of the people of God, but in that first instant begin the discovery and the passion that will enliven the sermon.

The word *turn-on* provides an excellent description of the initial reaction. Obviously, the word has come into use with the discovery and use of electronic media. Most suggestions I have read or heard on preparation for preaching advise reading or brooding over the text for the sermon as the very first step. The preacher is advised to note "ideas" or "key phrases" or "concepts." *Turn-on* requires alertness to more than these essentially intellectual approaches. It does not exclude the mind, nor does it involve only feeling. It signals instead that something within the rich reality of the text has made a visceral claim upon the preparing, reflecting preacher, bringing her or his whole self to life, as surely as electric power turns on an electronic medium. And the *inner dance* begins.

The preacher goes on to explore the experience of the turn-on, finds words to describe its cause, knowing that the text has invaded his or her unique complexity of memories, experiences, sensibilities, ideas. Why, the preacher might ask, does the text issue its claim upon me in just this way? What are the specific memories and experiences it runs before me? Where does focusing upon this turn-on lead? *At this point*, exegesis begins, including the matters of word study, context, literacy, structure, and the atomic dynamisms of our last chapter. Now, however, it will more likely proceed with a highly motivated and interested preacher whose final work will more likely result in a turned-on congregation.

An Example

Most of my reaction to the classic Epiphany text, Matt. 2:1–12, had come from reading about the Wise Men and their gifts to Jesus. The last time I read the text, however, it presented me with a visceral turn-on at v. 3: "When Herod the king heard this, he was troubled, and all Jerusalem with him." My attention was first drawn to "troubled." Startling as it seems now upon reflection, I had not thought to ponder how strange it is that a baby, any baby, to say nothing of the baby Jesus, would trouble anybody—beyond the routine "trouble" *all* babies can cause! Persons troubled as Herod was troubled are abnormal and perverse.

Not much more reflection was required before it became obvious that oppressive rulers like Herod are always in fear that they will be overthrown. History shows us a Herod little concerned beyond loyalties to his person and rule, a murderer at times, the historians tell us, even of some of his own family, unscrupulous in winning and maintaining political power. Obviously, to say nothing of a concern to protect his own kingship, one born to bring a kingdom of righteousness, peace, justice, and love would threaten him. I realized that the stirring of my passion came from Herod's obvious similarity to rulers of our contemporary scene. Whether it is politicians, groups with special interests, or office dictators, who always run the risk of being blind to the requirements of peace and righteousness, or gangsters and mobsters who have no interests beyond their own evil acquisition of profit and power, the birth of Jesus as king will threaten.

A deeper intuition made itself felt, however, as I explored the turn-on. It nagged me; I could not avoid the sense of something more that had invaded my ruminations. The intuition suddenly became articulate in the second portion of the verse where we read not only that Herod was troubled, but "all Jerusalem with him." The import of the verse cannot be escaped: the birth of Jesus disturbs even us run-of-the-mill citizens: preachers, lawyers, teachers, weavers, and plumbers, to name only a few.

The sermon on "The Trouble with Christmas" did in part declare the threat of the kingdom of God as embodied in Jesus to all oppressive authority, whether parents, deans, executives, dictators, police chiefs, bishops, presidents, and the like. More than that, however, it set forth the issue of a "war that goes on in the heart of humanity itself, within every one of us. Shall we choose evil or good? Truth or falsehood? Cruelty or kindness? Revenge or forgiveness? Life or death?"

PREACHING AND RESISTANCE
TO THE TEXT

Even among those denominations whose traditions had heretofore not incorporated it into preaching, use of the lectionary has much increased. For preachers in those denominations, as well as in those whose traditions have always required use of the Sunday lections, a strong challenge has arisen from the failure of the lections of a specific Sunday to bring the preacher to life in what I have been discussing as a *turn-on*. Our response to the failure of a turn-on to manifest itself was suggested by the friend whom I earlier quoted with his "What is wrong with dull preaching?" Those were in fact his words in the context of a discussion concerning lectionary work. In his opinion, obligatory use of the lections for a given sermon should prevail, even if the sermon had little emotional fuel to ignite the preacher to responses in a way that might reflect an inner dance. The advantages of such obligatory lectionary use were more important. No matter if preparation must begin with the tired sigh of "How shall I preach on one of *these*?" The "discipline" of the lectionary would keep us off our theological or ethical hobbyhorses and prevent us from neglecting the "round" of Christian doctrine in favor of our personal interests, however valid, or our personal hang-ups.

I have no doubt of the value, for reasons cited, of the discipline involved in use of the lectionary in preaching. I have come, nevertheless, to the decision that, other values notwithstanding, I will never again enter the pulpit to preach upon a passage of Scripture, including the lections for the day, that did not initiate in me that visceral reaction I have been calling a turn-on. The unsurpassable Phillips Brooks of over a hundred years ago still speaks truth, lectionary loyalty to the contrary. One will, he declared, "preach best about what he at that moment wishes to preach about . . . the personal interest of the preacher is the buoyant air that fills the mass and lifts it."

Difficulties to the turn-on in the lectionary texts should not, however be overemphasized. Most of us have experienced the thrill of having a text whose relevance to the forthcoming Sunday morning situation was quickly sensed. Nor should we forget that instantaneous turn-on is not the issue. One needs often to keep sounding out passages of Scripture until a dimension of truth makes itself felt and stirs in the preacher once more the deep wish to sound out the Word of God. Nevertheless, one further route to discovery that may turn the preacher on lies in asking oneself, why does a specific text *not* turn me on? Probing the resistance may be powerfully motivating.

I recall in this connection a Sunday lection from Ephesians, the New Testament letter in which doctrines of the church form the substance of the letter. One might even say it is the New Testament statement concerning the church par excellence. That had made no difference to me. I had decided to preach on that lection because I had neglected focusing upon the church for some time, and none of the others sparked any interest whatsoever. The weekdays came and passed relentlessly, and no passion stirred in me as a result of probing the text itself, or reading commentaries on it and the like. No other work or document on the church seemed interesting to me or important. No ecclesiastical hero of the church beckoned from the past or the present. I consulted another minister, talked with my wife, but to no purpose. By 2 A.M. Sunday, I was frantic, thinking I would have to plead an emergency and find a substitute preacher early the next morning to take my place. That settled, I went to sleep, bewildered that nothing about the church as a whole or a text from one of Scripture's preeminent statements about the church cried out for utterance. Then, sometime in the wee, dark hours of that Sunday morning, the astonishingly simple question slipped into my mind, Why does the text on the church *not* turn you on? The question released a flood of emotions, and by daylight and with the lubrication of breakfast coffee, the sermon had arranged itself with the text generating in me the passion of a new experience of its power.

I began the sermon by sharing with the congregation my initial, vapid reactions to the Epistle text of the day. I speculated on answers as to why so simple a question as "why not?" should have been so slow in coming. Could one explain it by *loyalty* that made me hesitate to criticize the church? *Guilt* at daring to admit that it was often a corrupt though supposedly holy institution? *Fear* that my hearers would not like having an institution they loved brought into disrepute? Whatever the specific cause, I shared with the congregation that my excitement with preaching on a biblical text which dealt with the meaning of the church had to begin with my anger and frustration with the church, crammed into a dark closet of my preacher's career in the household of faith. I spoke to them of my former youthful idealism, my call to the ministry, my commitment to the church, how happy I had been at first to look toward work within it. But, over the years—and in facing the task of this sermon, I explained—I had come to grips with my disillusionment and faced the hard questions of whether or not the church even had any reason for being: Why the church—when it had practiced, sanctioned, and even promoted racism, sexism, sometimes agism? Why—when its ministers had done illegal and immoral things? Just like everyone else, many had committed adultery, neglected their duties, been slothful, lazy, incompetent. Its bishops had often lied, its popes had sometimes ignored matters of justice and oppression, all of them cheered on ardently by its laity. Why—though hardly a war in the history of humanity had gone unblessed by the church? It had often sanctified torture and all but worshiped ignorance. A typical portfolio of church investments had often revealed the church's willing participation in every known economic and corporate crime. Why the church—when in John 3:16 we are told Jesus was given because God loved the *world*. The church was *not* his purpose in coming, and one message to the self-assured religious folk of Jesus' time declared that God could raise up children of Abraham from the very stones lying on the ground (Matt. 3:9).

Together in this fashion the congregation and I groped toward the resolution of "why the church?"—a question that had had its beginning in my wondering why the text had *not* turned me on. No doubt assisted by the intensification of my own aroused self, the sermon had arranged itself with the repetition of the question as the leading theme of its first half and provided the suspense for the next portion of the sermon that included Eph. 1:4–5, which proclaims the purpose of the church in God's plan as involving the fact that "he chose us in him [i.e., Christ] before the foundation of the world . . . destined us in love to be his sons through Jesus Christ." The author dared, I pointed out, to link the church with the creation of the world! "Why the church?" is for the Christian like asking why trees exist, or why the sky is, or where human tears come from, or why babies get conceived and born. Among other things, the sermon's second part, in a kind of antiphon to the first, explored the church as a mystery in God's way of loving the world and how we have been chosen and destined to belong to it.

The sermon closed with an invitation to the congregation to brood for a moment upon the actuality of their presence in worship and then to look around the sanctuary and ponder how even such sometimes weak, often burdened, possibly corrupt and sinful persons as we were mysteriously called to the destiny of being God's chosen people.

An exploration of one's failure to experience a turn-on of passion upon a reading of lectionary texts may not succeed. My own choice, and advice to others at such times—and I do not believe they will often come—is to use some other way of preaching so long as one can be true to the gospel, which, as Dorothy Sayers once stressed, may be called "exhilarating," "devastating," or "rubbish," but not "dull."[11] I would rather be true to the gospel as a whole, proclaiming it out of the energy of discovery instead of casting a pall of boredom over it because of faithfulness to a text that for *me* and *at that time* comes across as boring and dull. Let the preacher hunt, not for an idea, but for the gift of his or her own excitement and feeling. Elsewhere I have remarked that our current culture does not lack for sensation. The call to preach does not require us to compete with that culture, but we can search for the sources of excitement in what first burst gloriously over the world as "good news." Such a search cannot possibly be futile or irresponsible to the good news itself.

PASSIONATE EXPRESSION

Preaching in the Spirit and power will resonate in what Paul called the "temple of the Holy Spirit" (1 Cor. 6:19). In this connection use of that phrase with which Paul described the body is not so strange as it may at first seem. The body constitutes the most basic instrument of communication available to the preacher. Words are produced and resonate in the preacher's flesh, bone, muscle. Expression involves the use and sound of the preacher's voice, lips, tongue, and movements that may well include head, eyes, walk, gestures. In one such manner, too, does the Word that became flesh in Christ become flesh in us. This is why on a very deep, though not readily apparent level, a connection obtains between the sexual promiscuity Paul was criticizing in the Corinthian correspondence and sermon preparation. Sins of the "spirit"—lust, jealousy, greed, hate—if they are "acted out" require the flesh, which explains how in the biblical perspective sins of the "flesh" are really sins of the "spirit" and vice versa. We are *whole* persons, each with spirit inextricably related to the body, both of which in a very real sense, for good or ill, are and function as a single entity. The production of the sermon in the Spirit and power will thus manifest in a different and wholesome fashion the spirit-body union.

The challenge the preacher faces here includes an appropriate and meaningful connection between *discovery* and *passion* and the preacher's voice, body, bearing, style of delivery in general. In this sense an enlargement of Saint Anselm's classic formula is suggestive. Anselm declared that thought is "faith seeking understanding." *Understanding* in the formula translates his word *intellectum*, involving the use of one's intellectual capacities in faith: defining and exploring concepts, ordering thought. In preaching, the classic formula can be used but revised as "faith seeking expression" in the only instrument the preacher has, that body which is the temple of the Spirit. An incident in a class on delivery illumines the matter.

Jim stood up to read Psalm 139. A regular-looking young man, mid-twenties, heavy, powerful in bearing, and a big, very fine voice. He held the Bible from which he read in one hand, looked out and smiled at us, then began to read. As I recall his performance, I think more than anything else of his smile: cherubic because of his round face. The active verbs of the psalm describing the activity of God in relation to the psalmist seemed almost to give Jim unmitigated delight: "searched," "known," "beset behind and before," and so on. His big voice rose and fell but always in delight. By the time he reached the closing verse he seemed almost to have a smirk on his face with his ever-present smile.

I looked around and felt that others in the class shared my discomfort. It took us awhile to discover the source of it and for the class to risk sharing our discomfort with Jim. Our discussion can be summed up here.

Jim's smile and the delight in his voice simply called into question above all the incalculable greatness of God—Yahweh, as many of us have learned to name God in the language of the Old Testament. *No awe was expressed!* Jim acted as though the three to four hundred years of "modernism" that had made faith in God so problematical for so many people had not transpired. Not only was awe missing in Jim, as engendered by the incalculable greatness of One who had brought slaves out of Egypt and continued the work of liberation, but also the awe of a man like Jim who is yet able to believe despite the powerful objectives of modernism to belief in God.

Jim also acted as though to be searched and known by God was always pleasant. The closing verses of Psalm 139 may suggest a fearful edge to one's desire for God's searching!

Jim's reading also unveiled an immaturity. He was so very familiar with God! Not intimate but familiar. Maturity would acknowledge that, even for one who was a primitive Hebrew, belief in God has never been simple: that the longer one lives, the more one suffers, doubts, learns to believe against many odds, and experiences the overwhelming greatness of the Searcher.

All in all, Jim's smile and the easy familiarity of his voice violated the hard facts associated with "knowledge too wonderful" (Ps. 139:6). He smiled away the vastness of the Creator-Redeemer's power, long centuries of tortuous doubt, the wisdom and experience of generations.

Work in the class did not center upon the causes behind Jim's inappropriate smile. That was for another time and place. It was important, however, that he learn how to express in voice and body the reality being communicated in the language of the text. Proclamation of a sermon based on a text requires such expression as well as a reading of the text itself. The preacher in a very real sense has as his or her task to *connect* the reality symbolized in the words of the sermon with their expression in the preacher's oral delivery. Otherwise, the situation is as though *fire* were being uttered in a calm voice when in fact one's house is burning down. Not the mere *use* of words, to remind ourselves of Dr. Parker's admonition again, but *fire* makes the difference between one preacher and another. *Fire* in this sense definitely includes the way words are said in response to the preacher's discovery over and over again of the reality of the gospel. Time after time after time, one preacher or another has managed to kill the emotional excitement called for by the language of the sermon or, as we saw with Jim in the reading of Scripture, overwhelm or, at the very least, obscure more appropriate emotional response.

To turn specifically from voice to gesture, the inner dance, to which we have previously referred, may find its outward expression in a gesture of hint. I use the word *hint* to distinguish pulpit gesture from the full movements that might be required of a character on stage or from those histrionic displays that may betray the preacher's yearning for effect rather than communication of a discovery. If one, for example, has cause to speak of the fact that "Jesus trudged to Calvary carrying the weight of all the world's sin," *trudged* does not require a trudging up the aisle or across the chancel. A simple movement or two of the preacher's shoulders, suggesting the weight upon Jesus of the Roman cross and our sins, will probably suffice.

Let it be emphasized that no one way of expressing in voice or gesture can or should be required. *Fire* does not always require a shout so far as expression in a sermon goes. One person shuts one's eyes against tragedy, another may cover one's face with both hands. The voice and movement conveying language, which holds within itself the preacher's path to discovery of gospel truth, are as rich and colorful in variation as all the preachers who speak. The one necessary ingredient is a sense by the listening congregation of appropriateness as defined by the discussion we have carried on in these pages.

Passionate expression is a complex, fascinating, and indeed mysterious process. It involves, as we have seen, matters of great concern long before Ronald Reagan, a former movie actor, became president of the United States. Nevertheless, compliments often given him by both devotees and detractors for his abilities as a "communicator" have dramatically underscored for us the concern of this chapter: that our *expression* of content affects its reception by an audience, as well as our *understanding* of it. Passionate expression in its simplest definition refers to the gospel as manifested in the quality of the preacher's sound and movement—in the "temple of the Holy Spirit." And I am almost overwhelmingly convinced that even as the cause—even a righteous cause—of a head of state may fail or go lacking because it was improperly, if not to say impassively, expressed, so may our faith as preachers be strong and substantive but lacking in that vital dimension of passion pleaded for even by our forefathers. When we preachers, however, have pondered and discovered the reality of that gospel given us to preach from faith's sacred texts, have come alive to it, and have let it resound in ourselves, it shall go forth from us in words full of the Spirit and power.

NOTES

1. Jonathan Edwards, *The Complete Works* (New York: Lavitt & Allen, 1855), 3:335, 336.

2. Ibid., 2.

3. We need not worry overmuch that for Edwards "the word affection appears to convey a more extensive idea than the term passion" (ibid., 3). Obviously, as there indicated, he did not intend to eschew passion as such but to include it. In this chapter I find little need to make the distinction and assume Edwards's general remarks regarding affections to refer as well to passion.

4. Ibid., 16. For the record, Edwards tries to ground the connection in Scripture by referring to 2 Peter 1:12–13.

5. Batsell Barrett Baxter, *The Heart of the Yale Lectures* (New York: Macmillian Co., 1947), 48.

6. Ibid., 49, 50, 51.

7. Halford E. Luccock, *Communicating the Gospel* (New York: Harper & Brothers, 1954), 69–70. Italics mine.

8. Kyle Haselden, *The Urgency of Preaching* (New York: Harper & Row, 1963), 21.

9. William Shakespeare, *Julius Caesar,* act 3, scs. 1,2.

10. John Osborne, *The Entertainer* (Chicago: Dramatic Publishing Co., 1959), 75.

11. Dorothy Sayers, *Creed or Chaos?* (London: Methuen & Co., 1954), 5.

3
Artistry of Form

Over and above all rules and resources of interpretation later acquired, I had learned in this instance to respect the naked text itself, to let the word and the words have their own untrammeled course, to be open to their deeper signals, to let the naïf speak to the naïf and depth to depth. (Amos Wilder, *Jesus' Parables and the War of Myths*)[1]

It was like a piece of music. (A letter about a sermon)

A CRITIQUE OF PROPOSITIONAL PREACHING

Saying what a poem means is quite different from breaking into poetry. An attempt to state the meaning of a poem in words other than the poem's words may be expected, for it comes of reflection, which is a normal human enterprise. Moreover, we may not ascertain all a poem means unless someone more qualified tells us. Everyone has read or heard a poem that is difficult to understand, and an interpretation of it can be helpful. Nevertheless, the moment arrives when the poem itself must have a hearing if we are to know as much as possible of what it means. For a poem always means more than what can be said *about* it. It secures its full meaning within itself. If one could say all that a poem means without voicing the poem itself, to what purpose would the poem exist? As Wallace Stevens put it—poetically—"The poem is the cry of its occasion / Part of the res itself and not about it."[2]

A similar discussion has strongly figured in the approach to the artistic design of the sermon in recent years. For at least a century and perhaps even longer, preachers have tended to organize their sermons into what we might describe as *propositional* form, or, to use a more traditional word, *points*. An old joke still amuses of the preacher as one who deals in "three points and a poem." The propositional form has rarely, if ever, required a specific number of points, but no less than two and no more than four are customary. In every instance a good propositional sermon must be well-organized, or, as my favorite word as a young homiletics teacher had it, *coherent*. Coherence might involve the treatment of a single theme or idea, a point at a time, until its conclusion. Or it might consist of what in fact are two or more major ideas shaped in such a way as to fit together into one sermonic structure, a structure that has earned the scorn of some homileticians. Like a homiletical David Hume, they declare that any logical connection between the points of such a sermon exists only in the mind of the preacher and upon careful analysis will fall apart like an ill-designed house.

Various factors can explain why the propositional form of sermon has thus come under criticism. Two factors may be interrelated. The impact of mass media, especially television, upon the way congregations take in information or view artistic form constitutes the first. Propositional preaching has tended to manifest itself in the sequential, linear style of a manuscript. Point, as we earlier noted, follows point, paragraph follows paragraph, sentence appropriately follows sentence. As such, various propositional sermons often manifest a remarkably similar design, on the model of a well-constructed magazine article, designed for reading as well as for utterance. My own teacher, George Buttrick, himself a master of the propositional form, advised his students to keep the "pages" belonging to each main point roughly equal; certainly, point one should ordinarily have less, for example, than point three.

A sermon in propositional form operates well in manuscript culture, that is, when the predominant method of arranging and receiving information consists of reading and writing. However, the expansion of the electronic experience—Marshall McLuhan in earlier days spoke of the electronic "galaxy" to convey the cosmic proportions of its impact—has meant that we are coming increasingly to face congregations who live and function in an environment where orality is, if not predominant, at least as pervasive as print. Other artistic forms of the sermon have now claimed the attention of preachers who live and function in that environment, to say nothing of their hearers, who, in the experience of many preachers, have often seemed to grow restive with typically propositional arrangements.

Which brings us to the second related factor: a fresh and broadened awareness, stimulated by electronic, oral culture, of the forms and shapes taken by the New Testament proclamations of the gospel. As Amos Wilder put it:

> The Christian movement was creative in various ways, including the phenomena of human discourse. This impluse brought forth not only new vocabulary and oral patterns but also new literary forms and styles.[3]

Since Wilder wrote those words, an enormous amount of other work has been done on the linguistic characteristics of the biblical material—of such enormity in fact as to boggle the mind of working pastors.

We may speculate that living in the electronic galaxy has provoked sensitivity and study of the linguistic features of our faith's earliest proclaimers, which, in any case, would almost inevitably invite attention to how those features relate to preaching. If, as it has been observed, the New Testament offers a verbally artistic treasure—stories, letters, parables, songs, doxologies, dialogues (which include the bracing dialogue of the diatribe form) proverbs, imagined historical discourses—then alternatives to the artistry of propositional sermons would surely claim consideration.

A third factor in this discussion may also include media consciousness and shapes of New Testament language, but it would stand consideration upon its own merit. It brings us more directly, furthermore, to the analogy we began with of the difference between talking *about* a poem and breaking into poetry. To pronounce a verbal meaning of what a poem refers *to* differs from being caught up in the poem itself, hearing and speaking its language, being seduced by its rhythms and communicating them, inspiring and lifting others by the utterance of it. Only by at last hearing the poem itself do we experience its full reality and power.

Sermons preached in demonstration of the Spirit and power are not poems, though at times they may contain them. Nor must all such sermons be poetic in style. But the analogy is helpful to our understanding. Sermons may be weakened if they speak at one remove from their subject by talking more *about* the gospel than communicating it more directly, which is precisely the danger propositional preaching runs. The preacher may get caught up in the process of abstracting from a biblical text, that is, telling what the text *means* and in a form that presents an idea or ideas in the same way one presents the ideas of a poem without the poem. A "distancing" of the congregation and preacher from the text takes place. The sermon may then take an arrangement by which the text can be looked *at*, from which it may thus be possible to hold the responses of one's deepest self, the gospel becoming an item for reflection— marvelous item to be sure—rather than an inescapable and overwhelming experience. Any sermon runs such a danger, but in preaching propositionally, point by point, the preacher may discover himself or herself in an unwitting struggle against what Amos Wilder has taught us: "The Christian styles tend to evoke and restore the face-to-face encounter." He also shares Gerhard Ebeling's words in this connection that the Word "is not just a bearer of a *certain content of meaning which can be violated,* but a *happening* which brings something to pass and moves toward what it has in view."[4]

Now let it be urged in rebuttal that propositional preaching as we have briefly delineated it has been and can be powerful, especially in its use by master preachers, none of whom we could mention failed in recognizing the danger. What student of Paul Scherer, to name only one, cannot remember, as I remember, his fierce critique of anyone of us who might get "bogged down" in the "past tense" in a sermon. It was, he would often say, like being stretched on a cross, the past in one hand, the present in the other, trying to pull them together in a meaningful connection. An unnecessary effort, he would continue, and reiterate, "The biblical situation is your situation!" He was in effect trying, by casting the sermon in the present tense as much as possible, to minimize what I have identified as distancing from the text. For example, of a Pauline text one might say (our honored teacher would declare), "Paul is telling us in this instance . . ." Nevertheless, the danger of distancing in the propositional sermon remains and not just as a matter of time, as it seemed for Dr. Scherer, but also as a matter of form.

John Killinger has more recently given what I have named *propositional preaching* the phrase "developmental preaching," supported such preaching with insight, instructed us well in how to make use of it, and declared it to be the "workhorse of the Christian pulpit." Let a preacher use it if he or she wishes, acknowledging the considerable power that may accrue to any artistic form wherein the Word is preached. But new ways of preparing sermons constantly appear, and I am troubled by the insistence that the propositional (or developmental) form "has remained the best method of sermon preparation through the ages because experience has shown that it works effectively."[5]

Here from my files as illustrations are two versions of a sermon I have preached on the Prodigal Son (Luke 15:11–24). The first was in propositional form and titled "On Coming to Oneself" (cf. v. 17). The introduction noted how at times, as in a flash, we see ourselves and went on to remark how we are suddenly gifted in those moments with sober, cold self-awareness. We see what we have made of the precious life we have and what we might do to change it into something better. So with the young man in this parable Jesus told; then, "he came to himself." He saw why he had come to be what he was, and, more important, he saw a way out. We pay tribute to the parable, the introduction continued, when we say of someone, "He/she hasn't been him/herself lately." Or we say, "Get hold of yourself!" There is a brighter, truer self-knowledge, along with the requirements that issue therefrom. I am preaching this sermon today, the introduction concluded, in the hope that someone will come to himself or herself.

The three points that followed in the unfolding of this theme were:

1. *The young man came to see that self-fulfillment does not come of idolatrous self-seeking.* Its various expressions can be found in every generation. The urge for more money, more self-indulgence, more security—self-seeking better described as self-deception. For no person can live only for and by self alone. Even a hermit must seek substance from plants and shrubs he cannot grow, shelter from a cave he probably did not dig. None of us made it to halfway normal maturity without someone's love and care. We live in houses we did not build, read books we did not write, walk streets we did not pave. And the love we share with family and friends? Sheer mystery and gift! The children we gave birth to? Sheer mystery and gift! Eternal life with Christ? Sheer mystery and gift! No one owns life, much less her or his own.

2. *The young man came to see that idolatrous self-seeking had brought him to uselessness and despair.* "No one," says Jesus, "gave him anything" (v. 16). His friends were no less selfish than he. He "wasted" his substance. Do we not waste our substance? (Here the sermon gave current examples of our prodigality of our personal and natural resources.) Wasted dollars! Wasted thoughts! Wasted words!

What, it was asked, if we dare to face up to our sheer wasting of life itself? Then, we may be coming to ourselves, and a light is breaking!

3. So we join with this wayward young man in a moment of recognition and fulfillment. What a relief to get out of the pig sty! *He saw he belonged to some greater will than self-will, to a greater love than self-love.* He saw he was a child of God, a creature born of eternity. He saw that we are in this good world by divine invitation and that we "find ourselves" through nothing else but the beckoning of God.

Can we respond to this beckoning? Sin in these days may not only be expressed in rebellion and flagrant disobedience of the will of God. It may also be manifested in our laziness, dullness, slowness to reach up and out to the opportunities of God's will. The disasters of our time may not come from deliberate faults of character alone; they may come as well from cramped, little folk who prefer a pig sty to a Father's mansion.

Freedom in the gospel is not just freedom to do what we please but freedom to do what God intends and wants for us—like an eagle soaring off into the sun and undreamed-of heights.

How desperately God beckons is shown at—yes!—Calvary!

The conclusion declared that coming to oneself means to discover that we belong to God. Our true life is in God's mercy and grace, not in self-will, which leads only into an alien, distant land. To prodigals everywhere the message is loud and clear. Come to your senses! Get hold of yourself! Come across the fields to where love is! Come home!

The sermon in its longer written form—and it was completely written—has an intricacy about it, words and sentences carefully arranged.

Here in contrast is the second version, titled: "The Gospel of Breaking Out." It is not as easily susceptible to summary statements of points to be made as it is to situations to be described and clarified in relation to the gospel as declared in Jesus' parable. It was not written, but it was designed. The following summary is off a tape of the sermon itself as preached.

> I am thinking here of guilt, unhappiness, from major goofs that have run us into personal disaster, and we see no hope for the future. Catholics distinguish between venial sins and mortal sins. Frankly, I wonder about the mortal ones, even in such a nice crowd as this. Any murderers here or former murderers? Maybe. Thieves or former thieves? Probably. Adulterers? Probably. Probably, covetousness is present here, as are false witnesses, and breakers of all the other commandments. To say nothing of parents who feel like failures, children who also feel like failures, and both wondering, "Is there a future for us?" Even if our sins are only venial, they betray an orientation of self that often leads to worse and mortally sinful things. The fact is, we find ourselves locked in, like a prodigal: trapped by bad choices, major mistakes, incredibly shortsighted errors.

Here the sermon speculated on what leads us, along with the prodigal, into a "far country" and the experiences he may have had there, then declared:

> The good news for us as well as for him is that we are not locked in, not hopelessly trapped. No momentous goof can stop us, no guilt can defeat us, no mistake can deny us. We are children of God here, now, today, this moment, the doors once locked to hope have been broken down. We are released from the imprisonment of those terrible choices and freed to get on the road toward home!

This is not strictly an introduction, for it could constitute the whole sermon. It is a description of the situation described by Jesus with a few embellishments the parable attracts unto itself. In this sermon I continued with three vignettes summarized as follows:

> A young husband confesses to his pastor eleven years and three children after his wedding that he never wanted to get married in the first place. He feels trapped by his earlier choice.

> An older man in his early sixties is bitter, though he never talks about it. Putting the details together from here and there, one learns of a mistake he made thirty years ago. His wife has never let him forget it. For thirty years she has kept a ring of guilt through his nose and led him around like a slave.

> In the hair salon the other day, a young woman was trying to keep her three small sons in order. Why the tight lines in her face? Anger? Worry?

That fall upon it out of the wind. We seek
The poem of pure reality, untouched
By trope or deviation, straight to the Word,
Straight to the transfixing object . . . .[6]

A sermon can be sought just as a poet seeks the poem of "pure reality." The preacher, like the poet, keeps coming back to the "reality"—in the preacher's case, the text—that grounds the gospel message. As Stevens well knew, the intensity of such an exploration yields a new, fresh poem. Just so may the creator and maker of a sermon re-create the reality of that text which proclaims the Word of God, letting, as Wilder has said, the "word and the words have their own untrammeled course."

To return to the sermons above on the prodigal, the weakness of the first was in its statement of what the text *means*, necessitating a certain abstraction and distance, to which attention has already been directed. Whatever superior strength and power resided in the second came from its proclamation of the good news of freedom for the future, declared at the outset and repeated in connection with the three vignettes, each of which was a version of the prodigal's captivity. The one sermon declared a content, the other created the possibility of a sermonic happening.

WHAT DO I DO?

Artistry in the form of the second variety may more clearly emerge when the preacher asks not "what idea or ideas does the text provide me?" nor "what does the text call upon me to say in my language?" but "what does the text call upon me to *do* in my language?" I do not doubt that the responses to the questions will overlap on occasion, but the shapes of the sermons as a whole will differ considerably. For instance, in keeping with the theme of "breaking out" in the second sermon on the prodigal, the language (which included the repetition of the gospel message of freedom in the three vignettes) was designed to batter down locked doors.

An especially interesting challenge to the question, what do I do with language? is put by the story of the transfiguration of Jesus (cf. Matt. 17:1–8; Mark 9:2–10; Luke 9:28–36). The story does not tell of ordinary, human events with the historicity of other reports of Jesus' adult life—that is, many of his contemporaries would not have seen or witnessed it or found it plausible. That is why some have viewed it as a misplaced resurrection story or as a mystical vision peculiar to Jesus and certain of his friends. The account thus invites "ideas" as to its symbolic meaning, statements of what the transfiguration is *about*, what it *meant* to his disciples, and what in turn its meaning implies for us. One might consider how it reminds us of ordinary things we need to see or sometimes unwittingly come to see in their true perspective. Or one might speak of its implications for understanding the nature of Jesus, who is in fact the Christ of the Living God. A favorite—and true—admonition involves the temptation to stay on the "mountain top" of religious ecstasy, forgetting that discipleship means following Jesus into the common, often miserable life of the "valley."

When we ask what the text calls upon us to do in language, however, other possibilities suggest themselves. Noting that the text emphasizes a visual experience in its accent upon how Jesus *looked*, a preacher might decide to paint the picture, describe the scene. At least two commentators in my experience have indeed suggested using, in a transfiguration sermon, Raphael's painting *Transfiguration* for this specific purpose. How a complete sermon might be structured with the visual image in view would depend, as in every other sermon, on the unique creativity of the preacher involved.

The problem of such a sermon developed from the text in this instance continues, though the preacher would be asking the right question. The problem lies in the fact that the concern to speak of how the transfigured Jesus *looked*, even in the high artistic perspective of a Raphael, still puts distance between the congregation and the momentous statement the transfiguration texts embody. Not the least, incidentally, because visuality can place us at a distance, and it attempts to put the more intimate, sound medium of the preacher's voice in its service.[7]

My own last attempt to preach the transfiguration in answer to what the text calls upon me to do was: "To give expression, not just to the transfiguration scene, but to the transfiguration experience itself." To do that I found myself taking the entire service of worship as the context, or setting. The church sanctuary itself became for my purpose the mountain top of the text, the congregation the disciples. The sermon therefore began, "Here we are with Jesus; we are his disciples too, with our own needs, questions, desperation, confusion." After elabo-

witnessed it or found it plausible. That is why some have viewed it as a misplaced resurrection story or as a mystical vision peculiar to Jesus and certain of his friends. The account thus invites "ideas" as to its symbolic meaning, statements of what the transfiguration is *about*, what it *meant* to his disciples, and what in turn its meaning implies for us. One might consider how it reminds us of ordinary things we need to see or sometimes unwittingly come to see in their true perspective. Or one might speak of its implications for understanding the nature of Jesus, who is in fact the Christ of the Living God. A favorite—and true—admonition involves the temptation to stay on the "mountain top" of religious ecstasy, forgetting that discipleship means following Jesus into the common, often miserable life of the "valley."

When we ask what the text calls upon us to do in language, however, other possibilities suggest themselves. Noting that the text emphasizes a visual experience in its accent upon how Jesus *looked*, a preacher might decide to paint the picture, describe the scene. At least two commentators in my experience have indeed suggested using, in a transfiguration sermon, Raphael's painting *Transfiguration* for this specific purpose. How a complete sermon might be structured with the visual image in view would depend, as in every other sermon, on the unique creativity of the preacher involved.

The problem of such a sermon developed from the text in this instance continues, though the preacher would be asking the right question. The problem lies in the fact that the concern to speak of how the transfigured Jesus *looked*, even in the high artistic perspective of a Raphael, still puts distance between the congregation and the momentous statement the transfiguration texts embody. Not the least, incidentally, because visuality can place us at a distance, and it attempts to put the more intimate, sound medium of the preacher's voice in its service.[7]

My own last attempt to preach the transfiguration in answer to what the text calls upon me to do was: "To give expression, not just to the transfiguration scene, but to the transfiguration experience itself." To do that I found myself taking the entire service of worship as the context, or setting. The church sanctuary itself became for my purpose the mountain top of the text, the congregation the disciples. The sermon therefore began, "Here we are with Jesus; we are his disciples too, with our own needs, questions, desperation, confusion." After elaborating that statement further but in *such a way as to keep us in the setting*, I asked, "What is going on with him that brings us here, causes us to wonder at him, struck as we are with the power of his presence?" Here the sermon declared Jesus' oneness with God and spoke of those times when we were especially aware of his divine reality and how in our recollection the awareness continues.

If the task of the sermon was to express the transfiguration experience itself, a challenge further presented itself of how to express and intensify the ecstatic nature of that experience. It occurred to me in this connection to do what I had never done: to use the same hymn at the end of the service of worship as at the beginning. The hymn was "All Hail the Power of Jesus' Name."

Repetition, we should interject here, can express and increase intensity. One thinks of how the intensity of hymns with choruses increases as a chorus is sung after each verse. Handel's use in the "Hallelujah Chorus" of the repetition of "He shall reign forever and ever" and "King of Kings and Lord of Lords" and the word "Hallelujah" itself build to such unbearable ecstasy that, in legend at least, it brought a king to his feet. Some variation—the words of the hymn, for example, or Handel's shifting of notes to a higher pitch or adding voices—gives the repetition additional effect. The variation here suggested itself through a change of the tunes to the chosen hymn. For the opening, the tune was "Coronation," for the closing "Diadem."

The one last element in the design would require appropriate linkage of the sermon to the hymn. Prior to the singing of the hymn at the closing, the sermon declared:

So here we are today in the transfigured presence of Jesus. What an awesome moment it is! No wonder I felt inspired to sing the same hymn at the end with which we began our service! It reminds me of being with friends at a place one time and listening to a man playing the saxophone. Though it soon became obvious it was not just *a* sax, but was definitely *his* sax! He grasped it like a part of himself as he played it. He caressed it. He held it with love. He became one with it. And the music! He played and sweated with tenderness and labored over each note. He bowed low with his eyes closed, pulling music from someplace down below, way down. He bent backwards and called forth sounds out of the very ether to himself, sounds none of us had ever heard. He worked. He sweated. He played. He blew into the music of that horn the very breath of life.

Then he stopped a moment. In silence he collaborated with an invisible companion. Then he twisted his whole body and hit a high, high note, far off, and, at that instant, it seemed, he touched heaven.

There was utter silence. Somebody said, "Oh Sam, play it again!"

That is how we feel here with our Divine Companion, caught up in the rhythm and sound and ecstasy of his presence. We can't sing enough. It reverberates within us over and over again. And in such moments we are willing to leave this place with Jesus and follow him into every valley filled with the shadow of death. LET US SING IT AGAIN!

The effort must speak for itself. Note in addition, however, that the typical admonition "we must always return to the valley" gains power when put in just this way, while leaving the peak experience of transfiguration undiminished. Also, the sermon indicates how artistic design and passionate expression function together. The design of a sermon deals basically with how the sermon might appear on paper. Passionate expression deals with its utterance. But each affects and supports and works with the other. Indeed, one may be moving most closely into the realm of the text when the design of one's sermon aches to be preached aloud. Remember Wilder's words earlier quoted: "The Christian styles tend to evoke and *restore* (my italics) the face-to-face encounter." *Encounter* here means neither brutal confrontation nor lack of subtlety, but, rather, the sound carried and inspired by the text as permitted by the sermon's arrangement. If the text bespeaks ecstasy, let the design of the sermon permit the preacher and the sermon to resound with ecstasy; if a cry, then let the sermon and the preacher communicate a cry; if instruction, instruction; if narrative, narrative.

MOVEMENT AND THE TEXT

All literary or oral designs—a novel or a poem, for example—require a movement toward an appropriate finish. Sometimes, as in the transfiguration sermon just analyzed, the movement seems almost to take care of itself through the dynamics elicited by the text from the preacher's own creativity. At other times, the text itself may suggest a certain movement. One might think of this as a variation of the expository method of preaching, wherein the sermon takes the form of a running commentary on the text, verse by verse. Often, however, a statement of what the text *means* emerges in exposition, becoming an abstraction that runs the danger again of distancing. The variation of which I speak moves with the text and yet provides a new experience of the reality of which the text speaks.

Consider in this connection Paul's Letter to the Philippians 2:1–11. The sermon I have in mind—again, one of my own—spoke at the outset, as the text does, of the "incentive" and "encouragement" in Christ. Various and typical ways were mentioned in which different persons in the congregation may have experienced "incentive" and "encouragement" and "participation" in the Spirit. Do nothing, the sermon went on, quoting v. 3 as a rhetorical question, from selfishness or conceit, but in humility count others better than yourself? Without comment, familiar attitudes were recalled:

The fact of the matter is, Mom always loved you best. She never lit up when *I* came into the room.

Wait a minute, it was *Dad* who confided in *you*, looked to *you* more than he ever looked to me.

What d'ye mean "looked"?

I don't know, just the way he looked. And you talk about Mom and me? You *are* kidding, aren't you?

What? They elected *him?* When are *my* abilities going to get recognized?

They asked *her* to sing the solo?

George is *not* the best man for the job!

I think we ought to drop a bomb on every one of 'em, throw 'em in jail, run over 'em with a bulldozer!

Yes, the sermon moved on, "Count others better than yourself. Have this mind among yourselves, which is yours in Christ Jesus" (v. 5).

At this place in the text, the exegetes tell us, Paul inserted a hymn familiar to his readers, vv. 6–11.[8] For the preacher it is more relevant to say—nor does it contradict the facts of the matter—that Paul did not insert a hymn so much as he broke into singing a familiar melody, which climaxes at vv. 10–11: "that at the name of Jesus every knee should bow, in heaven and on earth and under the earth, and every tongue confess that Jesus Christ is Lord, to the glory of God the Father."

The sermon should share the same movement of the text. It would need thus to ring with the climactic music of the text. Chanting or actually singing the text itself would in my judgment have suggested sensationalism and overdramatization. Quoting a portion of the hymn, following the quoting of v. 5 above, with gentle attention in the speaking of it to its poetic (i.e., musical qualities) seemed sufficient.

Following the quoting of the hymn in that fashion, I shared the exegetical information that Paul was speaking to a divided church. I also noted that it is characteristic of Paul to go from speaking about a problem to an expression of praise. So here Paul notes problems, urges qualitative human relations, and then breaks into haunting melody. It is as though someone declares: This church is in a terrible fix. The choir and congregation are both divided, the preaching is poor, the people are unfriendly, the youth are worried, the old timers are depressed, the budget is tight. Let us all stand, therefore, and sing "O for a thousand tongues to sing, our great Redeemer's praise"!

The movement of the text and the attempt to have the sermon resonate with the ancient hymn led to the following:

Jesus is a marvelous one to think on deeply, says our brother Paul: "who, though he was in the form of God, did not count equality with God a thing to be grasped. . . . " To be honest, I haven't met anyone in over a year—at least!—who wanted to be like God. I have, nonetheless, met people who wanted to become president of something, to be full professor, to get tenure, to be soloist number one; persons who, in the *process* of wanting so much, forgot humility, service, tenderness, love, and whatever else blind selfishness and acquisitiveness can make us forget.

But, as we said in the beginning, we also remember Jesus Christ and his "incentives," what he has worked within us and empowered us to be and to do. In the midst of life's incredible problems we praise him. So! Rumble, you thunder, in acclamation! Strike with his Light, you lightening! Bark, dogs! Snort, horses! Chirp and tweet and trill your songs, you birds! Shake, rattle, and roll, you rattlesnakes! Sing choirs of angels, sing in acclamation! Sing everyone, everywhere, everything, that Jesus Christ is Lord, to the glory of God the Father.

ANOTHER EXAMPLE

When struggling to discern the *turn-on* discussed earlier, the preacher may sometimes discover that the specific text being dealt with is drawing a whole perspective to it, which in turn exerts its force in the shape of the sermon. An example in this connection comes to mind in a sermon preached on the Letter to the Hebrews 5:7–10:

In the days of his flesh, Jesus offered up prayers and supplications, with loud cries and tears, to him who was able to save him from death, and he was heard for his godly fear. Although he was a Son, he learned obedience through what he suffered; and being made perfect he became the source of eternal salvation to all who obey him, being designated by God a high priest after the order of Melchizedek.

Several attributes of the letter claimed attention as preparation of the sermon began:[9] (1) The suffering and death of Jesus, vividly recalled in v. 7. (2) The so-called Platonism of the letter in which a two-story cosmology figures prominently. The ideal, unseen, nontangible, world that is eternal, provides the pattern and meaning for the seen, tangible, temporal, real world. Hebrews speaks of the work of Jesus as priest, which goes on in the ideal world. To "see" Jesus (2:9; cf. 12:2) therefore has special meaning for the writer, especially since (3) the community of faith addressed by the author suffers from what one may describe as "tired blood,"[10] evidenced by their neglect of faith and worship. (4) The phrase recalls to us the importance of blood as a symbol in the author's mind. Jesus is the priest par excellence who gave his own blood in sacrifice, after the order of the Old Testament priesthood in which the priest offered up the blood of the animal sacrifice to atone for the sins of the people.

Out of these perspectives the decision on what to *do* in the sermon came quickly: to preach in such a way as to invigorate flagging spirits in the faith. The sermon began, after quoting an abbreviation of the text:

"Jesus offered up prayers and supplications, with loud cries and tears . . ." Many of us are here because our own loud cries and tears were heard, just as his were. . . . A remarkable thing and, then, more remarkable still, we were called to be priests to one another, both ordained and unordained priests, taking the cries and tears of others and laying them tenderly before God along with the sacrifice of Jesus. . . . The thing that saddens is our loss of the sense of the remarkability of what Jesus did for us and our call to mediate it to others. "Burn-out" has recently been a favorite word to describe it. A recent commentator puts it in the language of the Hebrews letter-writer as "tired blood." We know the mood: loss of faith, confusion of purpose, and no clear passion stirs our hearts, understanding goes sterile and blank. . . . I remember an older man from my younger days. He spoke to us, with a bit of condescension in his voice and a smile, of the idealism of younger men and, worse, of the idealism that

rounded" with far more than "a sleep"|[11]

I dragged myself out of bed one day last week, walked stiffly across the floor, looked into the bedroom mirror, and said to my face: "My God, it's Monday!"

And my face said to me, "Yes. And tomorrow is Tuesday, the next day will be Wednesday, . . . You like to quote Shakespeare. So, remember, 'Tomorrow and tomorrow and tomorrow and tomorrow creeps on this petty pace from day to day.' "

"Yes," I growled, "but only *three* 'tomorrows' are in that speech from Shakespeare." My face just kept on looking back at me. I in turn looked back; finally, I said to my face, "Why don't you smile?"

And my face said, "I want to, but you won't let me. You think only of sad things: a dispute here, a calamity there—to quote your Mr. Shakespeare again, you see only 'Woe, destruction, ruin, and decay.' "

I looked back, too amazed to reply.

"You know," my face went on, "what you could see if you would let me open my eyes?"

I kept staring back.

"You would see a special figure, a very special figure, arriving at a very special place—in time or out of time, it doesn't matter—so holy, so utterly holy that you would wonder whether you yourself could ever gain entrance into such a place. And that very special figure, looking like a bloody, whipped slave out of *Roots*, a crown of thorns on his head, strides in through the door. He grabs the crown of thorns off his head and throws it away like a boy coming into his mother's house on his way to a great feast, wearing a smile of victory—I said *victory!*"

"Now if you will just let me open my eyes," my face said to me, "I will *see* that and I will brighten. I will signal your heart to beat with great, steady rhythms to send blood everywhere; blood to your brain for thinking and imagining and dreaming. And I will send a message to your feet to dance!"

And I suddenly found myself saying with a grin to my face: "It's a deal."

And my face said: "Get outa here and on your way. Have a great day!"

SUMMARY

My appreciation for formal analyses of literary and linguistic attributes of biblical texts has been suggested. Preaching has much to learn from them, and I doubt that we have yet mastered all that such analyses can teach us. Meanwhile, the examples of preaching that this chapter provides have not emerged out of exact or slavish reproductions of rhetorical and literary designs deciphered by literary and rhetorical experts in biblical linguistics. Aside from whether the experts would themselves covet such slavishness, it would threaten to stifle the creativity of the preacher.

The substance of this chapter has sought instead to promote and encourage the creativity of each preacher to do what preachers have always wanted: to let the text speak for itself. Although all of us preachers have in general had that as our goal, our procedures often get in the way, muting the textual voice and diminishing its power. Our sermons too easily fall into talking *about* the text, not in bringing its truth to an expression undiminished in its primitive power. Careful and scholarly exegesis, lucid ideas, well-written paragraphs, brilliant discursive statements have their place in the homiletical enterprise, but without as much artistry as a preacher can discover, they can impede passionate expression, and, concomitantly, fail to produce designs that allow the text to speak without interruption, voicing "the essential poem at the centre of things."[12]

NOTES

1. Amos Wilder, *Jesus' Parables and the War of Myths: Essays on Imagination in the Scriptures* (Philadelphia: Fortress Press, 1982), 90.

2. Wallace Stevens, "An Ordinary Evening in New Haven," in *Poems by Wallace Stevens,* ed. Samuel French Morse (New York: Vintage Books, 1959), 148. Also quoted by Wilder, *Jesus' Parables,* 162.

3. Amos Wilder, *The Language of the Gospel* (New York: Harper & Row, 1964), 16.

4. Ibid., 24 (my italics). Cf. n. 2.

5. John Killinger, *Fundamentals of Preaching* (Philadelphia: Fortress Press, 1985), 52–53.

6. Stevens, "Ordinary Evening," 147.

7. Cf. the incisive discussion on the difference between sound and sight in Walter J. Ong, *The Presence of the Word* (New Haven: Yale University Press, 1967), 163–67.

8. Cf. Ralph P. Martin, *Carmen Christi,* rev. ed. (Grand Rapids: Wm. B. Eerdmans, 1983).

9. Cf. William G. Johnsson, *Hebrews,* Knox Preaching Guides (Atlanta: John Knox Press, 1980).

10. Ibid., 3.

11. William Shakespeare, *The Tempest,* act 4, sc. 1.

12. Wallace Stevens, "A Primitive Like an Orb," in *Poems by Wallace Stevens,* 140.

experts in biblical linguistics. Aside from whether the experts would themselves covet such slavishness, it would threaten to stifle the creativity of the preacher.

The substance of this chapter has sought instead to promote and encourage the creativity of each preacher to do what preachers have always wanted: to let the text speak for itself. Although all of us preachers have in general had that as our goal, our procedures often get in the way, muting the textual voice and diminishing its power. Our sermons too easily fall into talking *about* the text, not in bringing its truth to an expression undiminished in its primitive power. Careful and scholarly exegesis, lucid ideas, well-written paragraphs, brilliant discursive statements have their place in the homiletical enterprise, but without as much artistry as a preacher can discover, they can impede passionate expression, and, concomitantly, fail to produce designs that allow the text to speak without interruption, voicing "the essential poem at the centre of things."[12]

NOTES

1. Amos Wilder, *Jesus' Parables and the War of Myths: Essays on Imagination in the Scriptures* (Philadelphia: Fortress Press, 1982), 90.

2. Wallace Stevens, "An Ordinary Evening in New Haven," in *Poems by Wallace Stevens*, ed. Samuel French Morse (New York: Vintage Books, 1959), 148. Also quoted by Wilder, *Jesus' Parables*, 162.

3. Amos Wilder, *The Language of the Gospel* (New York: Harper & Row, 1964), 16.

4. Ibid., 24 (my italics). Cf. n. 2.

5. John Killinger, *Fundamentals of Preaching* (Philadelphia: Fortress Press, 1985), 52–53.

6. Stevens, "Ordinary Evening," 147.

7. Cf. the incisive discussion on the difference between sound and sight in Walter J. Ong, *The Presence of the Word* (New Haven: Yale University Press, 1967), 163–67.

8. Cf. Ralph P. Martin, *Carmen Christi*, rev. ed. (Grand Rapids: Wm. B. Eerdmans, 1983).

9. Cf. William G. Johnsson, *Hebrews*, Knox Preaching Guides (Atlanta: John Knox Press, 1980).

10. Ibid., 3.

11. William Shakespeare, *The Tempest*, act 4, sc. 1.

12. Wallace Stevens, "A Primitive Like an Orb," in *Poems by Wallace Stevens*, 140.

4
Caring for Others

Be near me, come closer, touch my hand, phrases
Compounded of dear relation, spoken twice,
Once by the lips, once by the services
Of central sense, these minutiae mean more
Than clouds, benevolences, distant heads.
(Wallace Stevens, "Esthetique du Mal")[1]

THE CARING ATTITUDE

Everyone was much moved by the sermon I mentioned at the beginning of this book, but a certain intuition about it would not leave me. I pondered it for months, listened carefully to later conversations and evaluations of the preacher, and came to the conclusion that, not only for me but for at least several others, something was missing. We had experienced great rhetorical power, but also a lack of power. What had we missed?

Then it came to me. After the meeting of clergy and spouses where the sermon was preached, lunch had been served, and I remembered that the preacher had eaten alone. I remember seeing him standing in the lunch line by himself, almost as though people were avoiding him. Having gone through the line, he sat down at a table and remained solitary throughout, almost, in my assessment of it, pathetic.

One could speculate that the power of the preaching we had heard made us stand in awe, feeling unworthy to get too close. Perhaps, some of us did feel unworthy. Or, perhaps, persons in positions of high performance or leadership seem larger than life. We know otherwise and avoid close contact with them to protect our illusions. The knowledge we try to suppress includes the knowledge that no one, even a great preacher, is really larger than life. Some of us may have wanted thus to enjoy our great-man fantasies, or he could have requested privacy after so momentous and emotionally exhausting a pulpit presentation. But the evidence does not support that he in fact made such a request.

The evidence gleaned from others and confrontation with my own deepest intuitions concerning one whose preaching I admired so much have led me to this observation: No one was "drawn" to him, nor did he in his sermon give evidence of being drawn to the congregation. We were impressed, moved, excited, awed, inspired, interested, amused, stimulated, bedazzled by the technical expertise of the sermon, but we still felt unloved, of little value to the preacher, bringing to my mind the words of Phillips Brooks:

> There is a power which lies at the center of all success in preaching, and whose influence reaches out to the circumference, and is essential everywhere. Without its presence we cannot imagine the most brilliant talents making a preacher of the Gospel in the fullest sense. . . . The power is the value of the human soul, felt by the preacher, and inspiring all his work.[2]

Some of us might be tempted here to quarrel with Brooks's anthropology (which led him to give a certain inherent value to the "soul") and the theological problems it would pose in years to come for more orthodox perceptions of sin and grace. But all that to the contrary, the acuity of the observation so expressed by that famous preacher of yesteryear remains.

One wonders whether or not, professionally speaking, we have recently given enough attention to such matters concerning the preacher's attitude toward those who sit as congregations. Attention has indeed been given to "communicating" with them according to psychological or sociological analyses of who they are and what challenges their characteristics and attributes as modern humans set before us. Analyses of this kind belong to what rhetoricians since Aristotle identify as *pathos*, which involves knowing the needs, questions, motivations of one's audience in order to persuade them. Surely, these characteristics are not foreign to a preacher's consideration. He or she will surely have them in mind and heart when shaping a sermon. But pathos as such does not yet embrace the distinction of that preacher-power Brooks referred to. A car dealer or political orator would do no less nor—especially crucial here—more.

Ethos, still following the tradition of rhetoric, comes somewhat closer to our current concern, for it involves the attributes of the speaker, including the speaker's credentials and credibility for purposes important to the audience. No less than pathos, ethos too requires our consideration. But, like pathos, it does not include the distinctive element that belongs to the adequate preacher in what Brooks called "the fullest sense."

Both ethos and pathos are included in the relationship between speaker and audience. The first signals attention to how the audience will relate to the speaker, the second to how the speaker will relate to the audience. But the relationship between preacher and congregation breaks the bounds usually encompassed in both. Only love, or the "value of the human soul" as Brooks wrote of it, or my own chosen word *caring* suffices, by which I mean a peculiar stance of the preacher toward all members of the congregation she or he addresses: a stance grounded in the love of God incarnate in Jesus Christ, but which, I dare to insist, is at the same time the preacher's own love.

Caring is a manifestation of that love wherein the preacher's words reach out to hearers, to "come closer" in Stevens's words, to affirm and shape their lives according to the message.

Caring involves more than pathos because the message may move against the hearers' inclinations and passions, and the preacher cares enough about *them* to take that risk. It involves more than ethos because it operates over and beyond, sometimes in spite of, the preacher's personal and professional skills and attributes.

Caring such as I have in mind not only signals our love as preachers for the congregation because of the gospel, it also causes us to admit that we offer them the gospel because it is the best, the greatest gift we can offer to those we love and pity and care for. Caring manifested itself, for example, in Jesus' weeping over Jerusalem; in Paul willing to be "accursed" for his Israelite brothers and sisters; perhaps, in Luke wanting to set the record straight for Theophilus; in the Ephesian writer calling out to "sleepers" to awake from the dead. It is an attitude more concerned with proclaiming the gospel, beyond ideas, doctrines, principles, and even artistry—which sometimes have, regrettably, seemed to be more important to the preacher than unique persons. The most brilliantly conceived sermon can be ponderous if it is not preached in a caring spirit. Even if it is exciting in the preaching, it will leave the congregation with an inner emptiness because they did not want to invite the preacher to table.

The quality of the preacher's caring does raise a certain theological issue. The New Testament does not attach much importance to the *kerux*, the herald. The kerygma, the message, of course, claims pre-eminence, the implication being that personal qualities of the herald, including a caring attitude, are in a sense beside the point. "Big-name preachers" do not really figure in the New Testament mind-set as essential to proclamation!

We are reminded here of the understanding that earlier developed in the church of the sacrament as *ex opere operato*, wherein the attributes of both the priest who dispenses and the recipient who receives the sacrament are essentially unnecessary for the sacrament's efficacy, provided its proper administration and the sincere intentions of the recipient in receiving. The tradition did not hold to the *ex opere operato* efficacy of the sermon.[3] But in the Reformation the minister was considered *ministerium verbi divini*, minister of the Word of God, and, however they might be explained or described, the benefits of the Word had as much objectivity for the Reformers apart from the preacher as the Eucharist did. If grace communicated through the sacraments did not depend upon the attributes of the priest, neither would grace communicated through preaching. Continuing in that tradition, Dietrich Bonhoeffer would hold that the "office" (*Amt*) of proclamation is more crucial than the proclaimer's personality, and he specifically discouraged less-than-formal relations between pastor and people.[4] That is, the attitude of caring (which in my own definition embraces affection, warmth, emotional excitement and attachment) would, to those who follow Bonhoeffer, probably be suspect or, at best (in the manner of the New Testament), beside the point.

Now the grace and truth of the preacher's message will always exist independently of the qualities and merits of the preacher. How could we even imagine otherwise? No preacher cares as God cares, whose caring is perfect and whose caring exists for both preacher and congregation, whether or not either *feels* cared for and, more important for this discussion, whether or not the preacher cares for the congregation. Were this not true, who of us preachers would not stand condemned and in despair? We are on every occasion of proclamation servants of a Word infinitely greater than ourselves, and referring people to that Word constitutes our paramount obligation and privilege.

But something else obtains as well, with unavoidable implications for the preacher. Our lives as a whole are inextricably mixed and manifested in our behavior along with our pronouncements, often either clarifying or distorting our hearer's apprehension of truth. I am remembering here an incident during one of my pastorates involving a very decent woman and a little boy in her church-school class. The exasperating thing he did or said does not now occur to me, but I do recall that she shook him angrily several times while exclaiming, "God loves you! God loves you! God loves you!" She spoke truth, but it was flagrantly contradicted, and, for a small boy, it was a truth no doubt overwhelmed. Although we would perhaps, at least in most instances, contradict ourselves less dramatically, we preachers may legitimately ask whether or not we are ever guilty of the adage, What you are speaks so loudly I cannot hear what you say.

John Knox put it incisively as he deliberated on the fact that "preaching is personal." He made it clear that for him "personal" included "how genuinely concerned we are about others, how eager to understand them and to help, how patient with them and how loving. . . ." He gave a humbling but accurate description of the dynamics involved in the relationship between preacher and people:

> Whenever I think of the men in the ministry who have helped me most, I think not of the gifted but of the good. Some of the good were also gifted but as I think about them, that is a quite incidental fact. Whether I knew them recently or years ago, I remember principally what they were, not what they said. In the pulpit, as well as outside it, what they really gave me was themselves.[5]

The independent status of the Word does not permit our avoidance of the fact to which Paul's classic admonition points us. Speaking with the tongues of men or women, or of angels, but without a caring attitude will make of the sermon only "a noisy gong or a clanging cymbal" (1 Cor. 13:1). Indeed, the theological truth of the Incarnation grounds this observation. The Word of God took shape in a life of grace and truth. The Word embodied itself. Whatever else ministry means, therefore, it involves modeling our lives, including our attitudes, upon that supreme embodiment. Being a servant of the Word encompasses far more than objective truth. It asks of us how we ourselves may be better servants of what our words and our voices communicate.

DISCOVERING CARE

As I said concerning passionate expression in chapter 2, feelings cannot be required. To command a caring attitude of ourselves in a preaching situation would lay upon us a burden of law we cannot of our own strength overcome. In this chapter, I assume the capacity and the will-to-care of the preacher, a caring for others out of the "services of central sense," as in the Stevens poem. No matter how skilled, whoever lacks caring, whoever cannot resonate with the caring of God as expressed throughout Scripture and culminating in the Incarnation, should not attempt to be a pastor or preacher.

Incapacity for caring, however, hinders us less than inattention to those factors that evoke it and fidelity to those many impulses and inclinations that first signaled our vocation. Let us take the instance of twenty-seven-year-old George (a fictitious name), who had joined a preaching group, from a small town in the South. He had the twang in his voice and the bearing of a "good ole boy," a style that at its best communicates warmth and affability and made George easy to listen to. But his reading of John 14:1–3, the "let not your hearts be troubled" passage, was doomed from the start, and it doomed his short sermon. None of the good-ole-boy attributes drew the attention of his "congregation"—the group. None of us doubted that he believed the message of comfort the text offered. He spoke it with a certain conviction, just as he delivered the exposition that followed it. The form of his message artistically speaking did not talk *about* comfort; properly, as the text does, George *pronounced* the gift of comfort there and then. But his reading of the text and his subsequent message were flat. But why? How could we help him?

Almost instinctively, I asked those members of the group who were willing to tell us of a major "trouble" in their lives. So far as they were able of their own choosing to level with us, it was to be a trouble whose pain and stress still challenged them. George, the good ole boy, and I sat there for at least twenty minutes, more and more amazed at the suffering present in one small group of thirteen, all of them other than me less than thirty years old. Three of them shared the anguish of divorce—the experiences of loneliness, betrayal, and loss the breakup of even young marriages can cause. Another told how at the age of eleven, she had faced her mother's suicide. Yet another revealed to us that he had once been told by his father that the father did not love him. It still hurt. A young husband in the group reported that he and his wife were dealing with her pregnancy, which neither of them had wanted, and they were agonizing over whether or not she would have an abortion. Neither had slept well recently, and the decision would have to be made in the next two days.

As the last word of the trouble sharing died away, and we sat in silence for a moment, I asked George to read the scriptural passage again and follow it with his sermon to "*these* people." This time the power of the old words struck as they were intended: "Let not your hearts be troubled." A relationship between preacher and hearers declared itself and filled the room with its presence. With the activation of his "central sense," George's good-ole-boy voice and stance softened. He could have shared that reading of the Scripture and his sermon anywhere! The "believe in God; believe also in me" became a gentle but strongly delivered command, mixed ever so delicately with assurance. The little sermon George then preached had the sounds of easy music flowing from his voice, striking and soothing those troubled hearts with the peace of Jesus Christ. We became participants in a sacramental and saving event.

My diagnosis for the cause of George's missing dynamic reads "inattention." Deeper analysis may lead us to harsher judgment, for inattention may itself be caused by self-centeredness that frustrates our caring impulses. George felt unworthy as a person and, by extension, as a preacher. He worried over how he looked, how he sounded, what "they" would think of him—all valid considerations when they serve the question of how we communicate to those we care about. But with George they were swept up into the raging vortex of his self-concern. Happily, the marvelous, beautiful gift of his caring when evoked turned him powerfully outward.

Other preachers in my experience wrestle not with feelings of worthiness, but with drives to succeed, to achieve, to be "good" or "great" preachers. They strive to preach right doctrine, they search the sources of passion, they shape artistic masterpieces—again, matters every servant of the Word should ponder—and the results can be homiletically brilliant. But if they are not also servants of the caring spirit, they serve a word that is not fully worthy of the Word of God nor worthy of the preacher's calling.

Perhaps, this is the most appropriate place of all to speak of the well-known "ministerial tone," messianic "ring" or "accent." The causes for that pattern of moaning delivery were touched upon indirectly in the chapter involving passionate expression. Unfortunately, passionate expression too can become the victim of that sound which turns a kind of pathos into bathos. But, although George happily avoided it, the origin of the tone lies in the selfsame self-centeredness that had impeded his first reading. For the ministerial tone says, "I want you to know that I care," which, being translated, really means, "it is important to *me* that you know I care, as how *I* feel about your feeling about me is more important than *your* feeling." The tone savors emotion for its own sake. It moans and groans with double-tongued selfishness. To avoid it, the preacher must really care—as George discovered he cared.

Our encounter with George further suggests that a part of our preparation to preach in demonstration of the power and Spirit will include a *care-ful* assessment of the congregation. A preacher of a bygone era recommended Tuesday afternoons for that specific purpose. He assumed that the text for the next sermon had been chosen. Think of the text for the coming Sunday, he advised, as you go from house to house, and ask how it could apply to the situations you visit. For me, that advice has come to seem a bit studied, even crass—a treatment of persons as "cases" for the Sunday morning task. The preacher had in mind, as I recall, that all-too-typical effort of preachers to kindle excitement which is too slow in coming, when the inexorable Sunday task ahead can seem so flat, stale, and unprofitable. The advice still contains some merit, but I prefer pastoral calling out of a simpler caring, uncomplicated by anxieties over the sermon in process, a caring that indirectly nourishes and enlivens the preacher's "central sense." Its usefulness for preaching will arrive in its own good time and way.

CARING AND SPECIFIC CONGREGATIONS

Not only will our caring include awareness of the specific troubles we dealt with in George's little congregation, it will try to anticipate the specific characteristics of the congregation at the time of the sermon. What may one anticipate to be their moods, questions, recent experiences on that occasion? One well-known preacher came years ago to a university pulpit as visiting preacher with a sermon on Lot's wife, who was turned into a pillar of salt (Gen. 19:26), only to be reminded that it was, by national proclamation at least, Mother's Day! Calendars and lectionaries may have trouble fitting such days into the liturgy, but, to say nothing of the confusion failure to recognize them would cause, the preacher who cares will at the very least take account of their importance for many, if not most, of the congregation. Those of us who, as preachers, faced congregations after the Challenger's fatal explosion could not possibly have as much effect without a response, direct or indirect, which took seriously that event of national import.

Most occasions for our preaching are, of course, more routine and liturgically arranged, but caring requires that the features of each should figure in the preacher's preparation. A short, private, written description of what one expects can be helpful. Here, for example, are three descriptions of my own, each of which was written as work for that sermon began.

It will be the Sunday evening beginning Holy Week. The hoopla of Palm Sunday morning will be over. Smaller crowd! Every single person there will probably have an unusual and strong faith. If some of them come because of strong feelings of obligation—law rather than gospel!— addressing the cause of obligation has more importance than the obligation itself. All congregations are special, but this one may be more special than others, it being a Sunday evening in spring, when most human fancies are turning to other than church!

School begins this week. The text that excites me is about wisdom! Happy coincidence! My challenge is to help the kids in the congregation—and parents—perceive I'm not another parent telling them to study hard and get good grades. At the same time, I, like most parents who will be there this Sunday, am concerned. The fact is I, like those parents, want to give these kids some *good* advice; that is, to preach 'em a sermon!

This Sunday coming up looks routine. I would expect an attitude that "this is a regular Sunday." Try to keep it interesting, but they won't be ready for a high-pitched occasion after last Sunday's worship. Don't

but apprisal, certainly not in the colorless sense of information, but in the pregnant sense of participation and communication.[6]

CARING IN THE SERMON

The preacher's caring will manifest itself, not, surely, in self-conscious, legalistic effort—such as we observed in mentioning the ministerial tone—but in voice and demeanor, in a personal presence which suggests the *preaching-with* we have spoken of. It does not require explicit statement. Nonetheless, a sermon can often find its beginning in such caring, a beginning one could think of as a variation of time-honored homiletical admonitions to begin the sermon in "life," or "where they are," or, as some have put it in more recent parlance, "inductively." The variation suggested here derives from the preacher's more specific focus upon the mood and setting of the specific preaching occasion.

Previously, I mentioned preaching to a Palm Sunday evening congregation, for whom the Palm Sunday "hoopla" was over and who were in church because of special, deeper faith. The sermon began on this basis:

We have come here tonight, despite everything else we could be doing, because Jesus Christ, the gospel, is crucial for us. We can't ignore him. We have decided we can't live without him.

Some adhere to other religions or, so to speak, worship other gods. Some are indifferent, it appears, to how or by whom life was created or to how and by whom it is sustained; uninterested in whether or not it can or should be redeemed, or how it will end. But for us these questions won't go away, nor can they be answered for us without the faith which is Christ faith.

We could be home writing checks to pay bills, or getting our gear together for a trip to the gym tomorrow to work off the weekend calories, or thinking about making love, or getting a head start on this week's work to come: Holy Week no holier than other weeks, just another week, without special activities, with few memories to share, without time for special worship. We could be home. But we are here!

We are the bewitched ones. We are the intrigued ones. Up against life's harsh realities, wondering, sorrowful, joyful, compelled to be here in this place, at this time, believing and worshiping Jesus Christ. The old spiritual says it as well as it could be said: "He touched me! Oh, he touched me!" With every variation of his touch as unique as each of us.

We are here tonight because we couldn't get him out of our hearts.

In the second situation mentioned above, it was appropriate to begin the sermon, not as in the beginning just quoted when a common mood was articulated and affirmed, but with the objection that I anticipated would be lurking in the minds of the youth upon discovering with the school year soon to start that the preacher was going to speak on "wisdom." The lection for the day and for the sermon was Prov. 2:1–8. The first words of the sermon were the first verse of the text: "My son [and it could be "my daugther"], if you receive my words and treasure up my commandments with you." Then:

> I can hear you both sighing and thinking: Here we go again! Sounds like it will be lecture number 613. The *full* one! The *long* one! Stuffed with aphorisms, platitudes, sentences, paragraphs, texts, gripes, advice, and proverbs.

From there, the sermon proceeded with a more accurate explanation of what I intended and how the text addressed all of us sons and daughters.

For the record, the sermon preached in the third situation above began another way than with an assessment of the congregation's mood. Which is to say that places in the sermon other than the beginning can express caring. We should be alert to those moments, both in preparation and in the preaching of the sermon itself, when, as Stevens put it, we want to "come closer," as though to lean over closer to our companion in conversation, or to move the chair we sit in over to the ill one's bedside.

Those moments may be discovered, as George did, when the situations of people take precedence over our own self-preoccupation. At other times, they may arise in desperation to communicate a meaning on behalf of the congregation we find ourselves loving. Time after time in the teaching of preaching, I have tried to bring this desperation to the surface by asking the student what I will often ask of myself: "What do you really and truly want to say?" The question can often push one to much greater clarity and activate the caring's "central sense." In the sermon on Proverbs the question led me to include a letter from a parent to a child, remembering that the letter form can convey caring involvement.

> I am not trying to ram my wisdom down your throat. It's something else entirely I have in mind. Let me put it another way.

In the second situation mentioned above, it was appropriate to begin the sermon, not as in the beginning just quoted when a common mood was articulated and affirmed, but with the objection that I anticipated would be lurking in the minds of the youth upon discovering with the school year soon to start that the preacher was going to speak on "wisdom." The lection for the day and for the sermon was Prov. 2:1–8. The first words of the sermon were the first verse of the text: "My son [and it could be "my daugther"], if you receive my words and treasure up my commandments with you." Then:

> I can hear you both sighing and thinking: Here we go again! Sounds like it will be lecture number 613. The *full* one! The *long* one! Stuffed with aphorisms, platitudes, sentences, paragraphs, texts, gripes, advice, and proverbs.

From there, the sermon proceeded with a more accurate explanation of what I intended and how the text addressed all of us sons and daughters.

For the record, the sermon preached in the third situation above began another way than with an assessment of the congregation's mood. Which is to say that places in the sermon other than the beginning can express caring. We should be alert to those moments, both in preparation and in the preaching of the sermon itself, when, as Stevens put it, we want to "come closer," as though to lean over closer to our companion in conversation, or to move the chair we sit in over to the ill one's bedside.

Those moments may be discovered, as George did, when the situations of people take precedence over our own self-preoccupation. At other times, they may arise in desperation to communicate a meaning on behalf of the congregation we find ourselves loving. Time after time in the teaching of preaching, I have tried to bring this desperation to the surface by asking the student what I will often ask of myself: "What do you really and truly want to say?" The question can often push one to much greater clarity and activate the caring's "central sense." In the sermon on Proverbs the question led me to include a letter from a parent to a child, remembering that the letter form can convey caring involvement.

> I am not trying to ram my wisdom down your throat. It's something else entirely I have in mind. Let me put it another way.

School days in the fall always make me a bit sad watching the earth in its downward cycle. The corn stalks in the neighbor's backyard, worn out with the heat and the fight against worms and bugs, turned brown several days ago, having lived their time. My roses are wanting me to cover them to escape the winter creeping in.

Not that I feel like tired corn or a scared rose! Nor could I get bogged down in thoughts of death if I tried! But! Nature cycling its way toward an end does give a melancholy edge to my pen as I think of how you are growing up, in some sense moving on, and away from us. And—this is the point I'm trying to make—I find myself having lived long enough to wish I had done some things better for you than I did and to wish I could give you something more for having loved me so much. I feel that I have so little to offer you beyond routine righteousness, routine goodness, decent parenthood, though every once in a while you could give me more credit than you do for having been a *little* more *un*righteous at your age! I wasn't quite an angel, was never as wonderful as your grandmother keeps telling you I was! Nor am I yet. Grandmothers ought to know better! (Not that I want to have outsinned you!)

I just want to say that the best gift I can offer, the only really great thing, far better than money, of which I have too little, or a car, which you can jolly well earn for yourself, or even a valuable education, is: God. Yes, son and daughter, God!

I cannot present God to you, of course. But I can point you to that Reality. I can turn you over to it in faith. I can remember you every day to that Divine Presence from whose love in Jesus Christ nothing in all creation can separate us. I can let you know that I really believe in that *ultimate* caring for you, which, even with all my love, I cannot give you, but which, because I love you, I am so deeply glad you can count on.

The fear of the Lord is the beginning of wisdom. That's the wisdom I'm trying to transmit here. It's the only thing, dear children of mine, that makes it possible for me to endure it when you leave my presence: and, sometimes, when I wake up in the middle of the night wondering where you are.

All my own caring,
Dad

The same expressions of caring in the sermon could become something of an issue, in view of some recent discussions of preaching. Some worry about being *too* direct, *too* forthright, in the manner and mood of the beginning of the first sermon above. A certain indirection of statement speaks, it is urged, with more power, such as the letter above. Overtones of the worry can sometimes be heard in discussions of the sermon as "story." Explicitly stated caring, the worry continues, can seem like smothering or coercive love in an age that cherishes individual, creative freedom. Members of the congregation prefer to "apply" the sermon to their own selves and situations, and they prefer such forms as would allow the preacher to keep a proper distance. Apparently, one may be expected to say "I love you" to one's spouse, but a congregation who heard it would be threatened. The earlier voice of a Harry Emerson Fosdick ringing from the Riverside pulpit with "Friend, listen!" or of a Buttrick—whom we met in chapter 1— more softly saying "I plea" at the end of one of his sermons would in this perspective be judged as obtrusive, interfering, rude, coming *too* close. One says what one *really* wants to say indirectly. In the manner, perhaps, of "I told this story once to a friend of mine" or "I once pled with a sinner and unbeliever to do thus-and-so for her own good."

Granted that caring in the sermon, like all good caring, seeks to allow that the person for whom one cares discover and develop his or her own potential and exercise his or her own freedom, I find the issue less important. At least, I find no reason to worry overmuch. Let the preacher discover sources of caring after the fashion explored in these pages and give expression as one's caring leads and as one's ingenuity provides.

CARING AND PRAYER

Prayer is the most crucial aspect of the preacher's caring. I refer to the private prayers for various members of the congregation, sometimes named in the prayer, sometimes not. We are touching here upon intimate, holy matters, not upon anything to be treated so casually as our quick "I'll pray for you"s often suggest. To treat prayer in this way as a technique is to me to act irreverently. One must work rather to discover one's own way, at times, perhaps, with the help of private, careful discussion with another who looks upon prayer with equal reverence.

Fosdick told us in his autobiography that "my silent prayer rose each Sunday before the sermon started: 'O God, some one person here needs what I am going to say. Help me to reach him!'"[7] In my own current situation, my office overlooks the churchyard. I stand at the window and pray for each one whom I see walking across the yard toward the narthex to enter for worship. Since my place of preaching is in a beach resort, many of my congregation are tourists whom I do not know.

They too are lifted up in the mystery of their namelessness along with the worshipers I do know.

However we perform the spiritual exercise of praying for our hearers, we are having to do with the power of intercessory prayer. Without it, even the most well wrought sermon, even one whose words declaim the preacher's caring, may fail. With it, even the humblest sermon by a bumbling, fumbling, inarticulate lover of souls may move the earth and heavens.

Only one other caring prayer has more importance. It is that prayer in which preacher and congregation unite prior to the sermon itself. All else ceases. We come forward to preach, and we say, "Let us pray."

The stillness following those words is special, like no other stillness at any other time, as we wait with the community of faith for the Spirit to "practise his scales of rejoicing."[8]

NOTES

1. Wallace Stevens, *Poems by Wallace Stevens*, ed., Samuel French Morse, (New York: Vintage Books, 1959), 118.

2. Phillips Brooks, *Lectures on Preaching* (New York: E. P. Dutton, 1877), 253.

3. Cf. the brief overview in Hendrikus Berkhof, ed., *Christian Faith*, trans. Sierd Woudstra (Grand Rapids: Wm. B. Eerdmans, 1979), 358.

4. Cf. the excellent Introduction by Jay C. Rochelle (trans.), in Dietrich Bonhoeffer, *Spiritual Caring* (Philadelphia: Fortress Press, 1985), 14.

5. John Knox, *The Integrity of Preaching* (New York: Abingdon Press, 1957), 60–61.

6. Gerhard Ebeling, *Word and Faith* (Philadelphia: Fortress Press, 1963), 326.

7. Harry Emerson Fosdick, *The Living of These Days* (New York: Harper & Brothers, 1956), 100.

8. W. H. Auden, "For the Time Being," in *Collected Longer Poems* (New York: Random House), 196.